MORE MUDPIES TO MAGNETS

MORE
MUDPIES
TO
MAGNETS

Science for Young Children

Elizabeth A. Sherwood
Robert A. Williams
Robert E. Rockwell

Illustrations by
Laurel J. Sweetman

gryphon house
Beltsville, Maryland

Published by Gryphon House, Inc., 10726 Tucker Street,
Beltsville, Maryland 20705.
ISBN 0-87659-150-0

World Wide Web: http://www.ghbooks.com

library of Congress Catalog Number: 90-81884

Design: Graves Fowler Associates

♦

To the children, grandchildren, and friends

who were willing guinea pigs

as we developed our new ideas.

Jennifer and Will

Jeff and Sissy

Susan and Janet

Amanda, Claudia, Katie,

Michael, Robert, and Teri

♦

FOREWORD

*I*n our workshops and classes with teachers, we continually discover attitudinal barriers toward science. Negative or insecure attitudes are expressed by statements such as, "I'm not good at science," or "I never liked science." Such an attitude begets the same from susceptible children as they model their teachers and parents.

As we query those with such barriers, we find that most, if not all, of what they learned about science in their early school years was obtained from textbook explanations. Gender bias also comes into play as they fall prey to the stereotyped assumption that males have a stronger aptitude for science than females. These factors, coupled with classes that emphasized rote memorization of facts rather than the wonderment of science that surrounds our daily lives, create negative attitudes toward science.

Young children have a natural sense of curiosity. They are constantly surrounded by events that motivate them to ask why, what, when, and how. If this natural curiosity can be merged with that of the teacher, the end result will be the teacher and child inquiring together with energy and excitement as they use the scientific processes to gather information and knowledge.

We want our children to be curious, to be eager to find possible answers to the why, what, when, and how. We do not want them to lose their sense of curiosity or their eagerness to explore. As mentioned earlier, many do lose this curiosity as they progress up through the elementary and secondary schools. Their curiosity needs to be nourished. One of the best ways to do this is to be curious with them. We cannot emphasize enough that teachers and parents can do so much by providing a model of curiosity and inquisitiveness that the children can see and emulate.

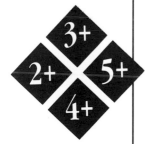

The age appropriateness given for each activity is an approximation, and is based upon our observations of many children who have tried them. Remember, each child has a particular backlog of experience which will guide any responses to an activity. The children and their reactions should be the final judges of whether the activity is appropriate for them or not.

ACKNOWLEDGEMENTS

We wish to acknowledge the following individuals who have made significant contributions to this book:

For review of science content
  Dr. David Winnett, Southern Illinois University Edwardsville

For endless hours of typing
  Mary Jo Peck

For support in all kinds of ways
  Cousin Jack Massey

For individual ideas
  Sherry Marti, Home Child Care Provider, Extrordinaire
  Joy Lubawy, Director, Campus Preschool, Wagga Wagga, New South Wales, Australia
  Jacqueline Williams, Environmental Engineer, Space Shuttle Program NASA
        (successful woman scientist and Bob's daughter)
  Barbara Goldenhersh, Early Childhood Consultant

CONTENTS

HOUSES FOR SNUGS, HIDEOUTS FOR HAMSTERS:
ANIMAL ADVENTURES

HOW MUCH, HOW FAR, HOW MANY:
MATHWORKS

HODGE PODGE

SCIENCE IS...

...Being a teacher who

- is growing and learning in the same way as the children are expected to grow and learn.

- provides science experiences that are appropriate to each child's development.

- asks questions and provides information that provokes thought, not answers questions.

- provides support if things don't go as they should, then continues to encourage children to try again or go another way.

- accepts children's ideas, challenges them with new ones, and causes them to test the accuracy of their own.

- keeps records on the children's progress and achievements so that every child can reach a maximum potential.

- collects science and nature things, and organizes them in increasingly complex ways.

- helps children organize data so that they can see patterns and change.

- recognizes science opportunities in all areas of the classroom, and integrates the science skills with other learning areas.

- provides outside resources such as field trips, speakers, or museums that support daily experiences.

...Helping children

- explore their natural environment.

- make discoveries about themselves and their world.

- sort out their needs, and search for more relevant information.

- learn more difficult tasks in a safe environment where they can make mistakes.

- learn by deduction, making discoveries through exploration.

- share their experiences and knowledge with the group, and learn to contribute to and use group knowledge.

- see the excitement of learning.

- share their findings with others.

- collect things and explore their relationships.

- find ways they can impact and change their world.

- ask questions, and then find ways to answer those questions.

- see that science can become a life's occupation or an interesting hobby.

- see that special materials for science exist and even a special language.

...Preparing an environment that

- is open to the outdoors.

- is safe to conduct experiments.

- encourages children to help each other.

- is filled with adequate materials which are:

  1. varied enough to promote interest.

  2. developmentally appropriate.

  3. scientifically sound.

  4. challenging to mind or body.

  5. both print and manipulative.

  6. able to provide opportunity to acquire firsthand knowledge.

  7. supportive of discovery, problem solving, and experimentation.

- encourages interaction with teachers, students, and things.

- invites children to return again and again.

- asks children to contribute information and materials to their learning.

- requires children to become involved in organization, upkeep, and cleanliness.

- is fluid and always changing.

SCIENCE CONTENT,
SCIENCE PROCESS

Young children are natural scientists. It isn't until they have been in school for five years or so that the educational system stunts all this natural inquisitiveness and drive. Can we define those natural skills better? Yes. Educators in the early sixties met and defined the skills of exploration we call science. It was necessary to classify these skills or science processes in order to develop a clearer understanding of how scientists work and what they do to learn to be scientists. Oh yes! We do learn many facts in our role as scientists, but most of those scientists would say that facts are subordinate to the **doing** that is required to obtain information. In other words, science is a participating, active procedure that can be defined for us by using the science processes, just as science content can be defined by listing the knowledge obtained during the activity.

What do the terms science process and science content mean to teachers of young children? It means that we should be aware of the different ways that these two parts of science should be taught. Science content, the knowledge of science, can be taught in a vacuum and just memorized. Many of us learned part of our science that way. For some of us that style of learning was painful because we needed concrete experience upon which to hook information that we were to learn. If we were lucky we learned science names and definitions in an active context where we applied each to an experiment we had done.

Thirteen science processes have been defined by scientists as procedures by which they go about their work. Several of the processes require high level abstract thinking, which our young children are unable to accomplish; however, knowledge of these process (work) skills of science by the teacher can allow you to develop pre-process or process entry skills.

You see we don't teach reading to 3 and 4 year old children, we develop their pre-reading skills. Just as in pre-reading, science process skills have entry or pre-skills that can be used with children to enhance their science success later in elementary school; that is, you can teach them to science.

Observation
The basic and most important process is observation. Using the senses of smell, touch, taste, hearing, and sight to record information about objects and events is the stepping stone for all future scientific achievement. While teachers conduct many observational activities during the regular year, the event becomes scientific when it is identified as science and when data is recorded for future comparisons.

Classification

Classification refers to grouping, patterning, ordering. By using observable characteristics, scientists organize objects by some attribute. Children naturally group objects; they select the food they prefer, the clothes they like, and the toys they use for play. Applied to natural objects such as shell, insects, and leaves, science requires logic to these groupings that can grow with continued experience.

Measuring

Measuring is the essence of scientific work for without numbers most information could not be transferred. Young children are generally unable to deal with exact measurements, but can begin to develop these skills by comparing and developing concepts of more, less, big, little, heavy, light, and others. Your bright ones will soon be asking for more exact measurements so you will want to have a ruler and balance in the science center to show them how to measure exactly.

Using Space And Time Relationships

Part of every preschool curriculum is the teaching of position words. Up, down, over, under, and beside are relative terms to any child expressing where they are in relation to other objects and people in their classroom. As they grow older and become more proficient in science, they will use these terms to express the position of objects in space, on graphs, and in motion. Time is a different, yet important, concept for young children to begin to experience. The teacher should involve children in events that show time use and change, because these events become the heart of scientific investigation.

Communication

Children at this early age are searching for communication outlets. They talk to everyone, even themselves. Science allows them to replicate activities time after time. The importance of communication as expressed in this process relates to communication that is observed in experience. This communication can be verbal, but also employs graphs, charts, maps, and numbers as well as models. Learning to be exact is a long way off, but practicing pre-science communication skills will benefit each new scientist.

Predicting And Inferring

Predicting and inferring are beyond the ability of most of our young children, but we can provide experiences for them where educated guesses can be made and tested. A child knows that a plant will grow and can discuss the event of a seed opening and the cotyledon and root emerging. The teacher can expand inferring and predicting skills by asking the child to venture a guess as to the growth by tomorrow or by next week. The key to the process is to note the observation, write down the guess, and, finally, check the next day or next week to see how accurate it is. Children may guess the outcome, but a scientist follows through the investigation. It is a great teaching technique.

Numbers

Using numbers properly is a must for the scientist, and number use can be enhanced in young children. The process begins when children note sizes, lengths, more, or less. The teacher can easily tear strips of centimeter or Unifix paper to determine size and size change by guessing numbers. While the young child may not remember or have a use for that value, the simple use by an adult tells the child numbers have importance.

Integrated Processes

Five integrated processes are controlling variables, interpreting data, formulating an hypothesis, defining operationally, and experimenting. The processes, to a large degree, are beyond the learning or involvement scope of the young child. We teachers, however, must know where our young scientists are heading and what skills they will need. With knowledge of how a scientist works and uses these science processes, the teacher can model good science in the same way that good reading, good vocabulary, good manners are modelled.

RESOURCES FOR TEACHERS

American Association for the Advancement of Science (AAAS)
1333 H St., NW
Washington, DC 20005

American Chemical Society
1155 16th St., NW
Washington, DC 20036

American Forest Council
1250 Connecticut Ave., NW
Washington, DC 20036

American Geological Institute
4220 King St.
Alexandria, VA 22302

Entomological Society of America
9301 Annapolis Rd.
Lanham, MD 20706-3315

Gryphon House, Inc.
Box 275
Mt. Rainier MD 20712
1-800-638-0928
MUDPIES TO MAGNETS: A Preschool Science Curriculum
HUG A TREE and Other Things to Do Outdoors With Young Children by Rockwell, Sherwood, & Williams (the authors of this book)
Write or call for a free catalog.

National Association for the Education of Young Children (NAEYC)
1834 Connecticut Ave. NW
Washington, DC 20036

NASA Headquarters
Code LE
400 Maryland Ave., SW
Washington, DC 20546

National Audubon Society
613 Riversville Road
Greenwich, CT 06830

National Geographic Society
17th and M Streets, NW
Washington, DC 20036

National Science Foundation (NSF)
1800 G St., NW
Washington, DC 20550

National Science Teachers Association (NSTA)
1742 Connecticut Ave., NW
Washington, DC 20009

National Wildlife Federation
1412 16th St., NW
Washington, DC 20036

Soil and Water Conservation Society of America
7515 Northeast Ankeny Road
Ankeny, IA 50021-9764

US Department of Agriculture
Forest Service
PO Box 2417
Washington, DC 20013

US Department of the Interior
Fish & Wildlife Service
18th and C Streets, NW
Washington, DC 20240

US Environmental Protection Agency
401 M Street, SW
Washington, DC 20460

Materials suppliers

Carolina Biological Supply Co.
2700 York Rd.
Burlington, NC 27215

Connecticut Valley Biological Supply Co., Inc.
82 Valley Rd. PO Box 326
Southampton, MA 01073

Delta Education, Inc.
PO Box M
Nashua, NH 03061-6012

Edmund Scientific Co.
Dept. 5556 Edscorp Bldg.
Barrington, NJ 08007

Frey Scientific Co.
905 Hickory Ln.
Mansfield, OH 44905

Nasco
901 Janesville Ave.
Fort Atkinson, WI 53538

Ohaus Scale Corporation
29 Hanover Rd.
Florham Park, NJ 07932

Ward's Natural Science Establishment Inc.
5100 West Henrietta Rd.
PO Box 92912
Rochester, NY 14692

Periodicals for teachers & kids

Owl
The Young Naturalist Foundation
59 Front St. East
Toronto, Ontario
Canada M5E1B3

Information on an abundance of different activities for the outdoors.

Ranger Rick's Nature Magazine
National Wildlife Federation
1412 16th St., NW
Washington, DC 20036

Provides activities and information to help children enjoy nature.

Chickadee
The Young Naturalist Foundation
59 Front St. East
Toronto, Ontario
Canada M5E1B3

Excellent for 3-5 year olds.

Your Big Backyard
National Wildlife Federation
1412 16th St., NW
Washington, DC 20036

Perfect for children 3-5. Wildlife photos, stories, puzzles, games, and poems.

Nature Scope
National Wildlife Federation
1412 16th St., NW
Washington, DC 20036

The Museum of Science and Industry
Basic List of Children's Science Books
compiled by Bernice Richter and Duane
Wenzel, 1986.
American Library Association
50 E. Huron St.
Chicago, IL 60611

START EARLY
WITH GIRLS TOO

*I*f you want to have good speakers, start early. If you want to have good readers, start early. So why not start early in science and mathematics. Research in the past 20 years has shown what happens when early intervention in any area is accomplished. Early years learning is clearly the most crucial period in the development of a scientist. Why then have we not paid more attention to this age in our teaching of science? We have not been worried about the number of scientists until the last few years as our country's scientific literacy deficit continues to grow. As this deficit grows, we develop a nation where scientific and technical use continues also to grow and companies scramble for workers who can function in these "science" oriented jobs. If changes are to be made, major efforts must begin with the early childhood curriculum.

In the same vein, a conscious effort must be made to recruit females, your little girls, into the sciences. Moving into the 1990's in Western technological countries, women in the science work force will account for only about ten percent. Researchers are attempting to define the cause for such a discrepancy, and the turn of the century will find us tackling the problem as our needs for competent scientists continues. What is apparent is our need to develop female scientists. Because those science habits begin young, the early childhood teacher's role in this massive effort cannot be underestimated.

Some things you can do

1. Have an activity hands-on science program.

2. Be a role model — be an active sciencer yourself.

3. Bring in science specialists from both sexes.

4. Bring parents of girls into the program when special aptitude is shown. Ask them to support their interest. Keep it up with the boys too.

5. Actively encourage girls who show aptitude in science. Keep encouraging the boys.

6. Make sure the girls have active roles and are not relegated to watchers and assistants.

7. Both boys and girls appreciate and feel the value of science when sound reasons exist for doing the experiment.

DEVELOPMENTALLY APPROPRIATE PRACTICE

*I*n their "Developmentally Appropriate Practice in Early Childhood Programs Serving Children from Birth Through Age Eight," the National Association for the Education of Young Children (NAEYC) emphasizes that children's learning activities and materials should be concrete, real, and relevant to their lives. In support of this emphasis, we have compiled a variety of science investigation activities that can be easily adopted to typical preschool unit topics and integrated throughout the daily curriculum.

Children are naturally curious — they become more curious as they grow from infancy into their pre-primary years. This book as well as our previous works, HUG A TREE and MUDPIES TO MAGNETS, utilize Piagetian theory. He, and we, feel that each child learns from firsthand (hands-on), initial experiences. Ideas become concepts as children construct their own reality, according to their own experience and information at any given time in their cumulative learning.

As teachers of young children, we must continually do things with our children, not for them. This means seeking answers and solutions together as we explore the wonderment of science. Sharing this sense of curiosity serves as a model of anticipation and wonder that can bring both children and teachers into a new learning experience. To initiate, to nurture this learning, is one of the most important roles we as teachers and parents play in interacting with children.

To obtain a copy of "Developmentally Appropriate Practice in Early Childhood Programs Serving Children from Birth Through Age Eight," write to NAEYC at the address listed in **Resources for Teachers**.

HOW TO USE THIS BOOK

*T*his book is organized in the same way as our two previous publications HUG A TREE and MUDPIES TO MAGNETS. The activities are divided into science content categories which are designated by chapter headings. By using the content areas, we hope to expose children to a broader spectrum of science than is usually seen in preschool classrooms. Preceeding each chapter is a discussion of the content area, how science helps us in our daily lives, and information relevent to careers in science. This provides teachers with some background information. A cross referenced listing of matching content activities from HUG A TREE and MUDPIES TO MAGNETS is also provided in each chapter. The chapters in the book are not sequential in order of difficulty; however, the activities within each chapter range from simple to complex.

This book has special features that enable the reader to use it without having had heavy previous exposure to science. Each activity is appropriately titled and is introduced by a descriptive paragraph. The "Language With Science" section lists words as well as ideas for encouraging the children to talk about the activities, ask questions, and respond to questions, all of which will serve to clarify or confirm their observations as they interact with the activities.

Following this is the "Things You Will Need" component. Here we list everything that you will need to conduct the activity. Most of the items listed can be easily found at a grocery or hardware store. Some items can be acquired from various resource people or specialty stores (see **Resources for Teachers**).

The "What To Do" section provides a step-by-step procedure. Remember that it is your role as a teacher to serve as a facilitator and participant, rather than as a provider of answers. You should allow the children to have an opportunity to explore, interact, and seek answers on their own. Directions are often flexible enough for you to adapt them to the needs of your children.

The "Want To Do More?" section is provided to assist you with ideas to expand the activity. The suggestions offered are usually more difficult than those found in the initial experiment. However, all are designed to build upon the foundation of the original experience. Many of these ideas can be used for an age range beyond the preschool years. They are suitable for primary grade children enrolled in public or private schools or for those in after-school latchkey or daycare programs. This section also includes some ideas for very young children.

COLORS, CRYSTALS, AND CREATIONS: CHEMISTRY BEGINNINGS

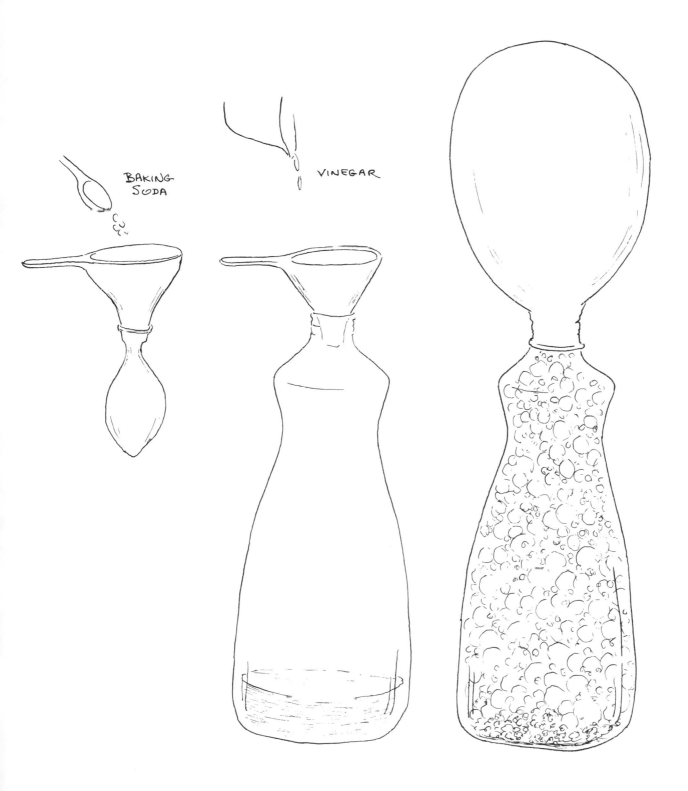

BAKING SODA

VINEGAR

COLORS, CRYSTALS, AND CREATIONS: CHEMISTRY BEGINNINGS

Chemistry is

- the study of materials, their composition or structure, and how they change.
- chemists studying and working with materials to understand their structure, make-up, and ways in which they change.

Ideas to share with children

- Chemists help keep milk pure, develop new candies and other foods, and find ways to keep food fresh longer.
- Chemists discover and create new materials for our use. The plastic toys and games you play with are different from the wooden or rubber ones your mom and dad had. The batteries that make some things work were developed by chemists, too.
- Compact discs, computer discs, and recording tape were created by chemists. The materials used in the discs had to have certain properties so the electrical experts could use them to store information.
- People use chemicals to clean, paint, fertilize, or fumigate in and around your home. Chemists made all of these helpful things.
- If you have been sick and have taken medicine, chemists have helped you. They developed aspirin, antibiotics, vitamins, and other things in your bathroom medicine cabinet.
- Some famous chemists are Michael Faraday, Robert Boyle, Demetri Mendeleev, E.I. DuPont, Rosalind Franklin and Neils Bohr.

Things to do

- You may want to bring some of the various chemical containers from home and discuss chemicals and chemistry with the children. This is a good time to discuss safety with unknown substances. Most hospitals have information on a poisoning prevention program for young children. They may have materials or a speaker who will make a presentation to the children.
- Invite a chemist, possibly a parent, to talk with the children about chemistry. Children will be most interested in equipment chemists use and things they do that affect children. Be sure your visitor enjoys young children. Tell the chemist what the children have done that is related to chemistry and what questions they might have.
- A chemistry laboratory can be an interesting place to visit, but visit ahead yourself to be sure that it can safely accomodate your group. You could visit the local high school or college chemistry departments. Given enough time, some chemistry teachers have some clever experiments that would be exciting for the children.

- If you want to focus on chemistry for the next couple of weeks, then get your white lab jacket out, put on your safety glasses and explore the world of the chemist. Old white shirts can serve as lab coats for the children.
- These chemistry ideas can be found in *Hug a Tree* and *Mudpies to Magnets*:

HUG A TREE   Tin Can Ice Cream

MUDPIES TO MAGNETS   Rainbow Stew
                                  Paper Chromatography
                                  Magic Matter
                                  Dunking Raisins
                                  Egg Carton Rainbows
                                  Shine Your Pennies
                                  Grow a Rock
                                  I'm Forever Blowing Bubbles
                                  Little Bitty Butter Beaters
                                  Good and Juicy
                                  The Purr-fect Smell

CRYSTAL POPS

Language with science

freeze
frozen
crystals
popsicle
liquid
solid
handle
melt
dissolve
cold
colder
hard

Encourage the children to think of their own words that tell what is happening to the popsicles.

Things you will need

paper cups
popsicle sticks
water
fruit juice
a freezer

When water freezes you cannot always see the crystalline structure that forms as it solidifies. Add some other substances, and the observable characteristics change. When fruit juice is added to water and frozen, the structure of the ice changes and noticeable crystal structures are evident. It is the "impurities" that cause the change. Just by thinking about science, a common summer activity becomes an experience that promotes language and observation skills. Encourage an atmosphere of curiosity and delight, and everyone will enjoy participating in the process from start to delicious finish!

What to do

1. Have the children mix water with a can of frozen juice. Pour the mixture into small paper cups (3 oz). Place the filled cups on a tray, then put them in the freezer. Also freeze a cup of water.

2. Look at the mixture about every 45 minutes. Talk with the children. Encourage them to describe what they see.

3. When the mixture starts to harden, remove the cups from the freezer and have the children place a popsicle stick handle into each cup.

4. Put the cups back into the freezer. Be sure to let the children see the crystals that are starting to form. Continue to check on the progress, talking about the changes that are occurring.

5. When the juice has frozen, remove the cups and give one to each child. Have the children peel the paper cup away from the popsicle. Observe the frozen crystals. Talk about the designs you see. Have a bite. As the children enjoy the treat, show them the water popsicle and talk with them about differences and similarities they notice. How did the water change when juice was added. What do you think will happen to your crystal popsicle if you don't eat it?

Want to do more?

Try freezing other edible liquids. Compare the different crystal patterns. Freeze bananas and grapes. Talk about similarities and differences. What happens when popsicles or fruit thaw? Are they the same or have they changed?

MAKING PASTE

Language with science

paste
sticky
mixture
suspension
experiment
formula
recipe
chemist

Things you will need

flour
cornstarch
water
spoons

containers for mixing (something small such as bathroom size paper cups helps control the amount of ingredients used)

paper

Paste is common in almost every early childhood setting. It is something that children can easily make for themselves. Making paste provides an excellent opportunity for children to take on the role of chemist and do, on a very simple level, the same sort of work adult chemists do. They ask a question, "What is the best way to make paste?", experiment with various possibilities, and come up with an answer. In doing so, they are using their skills to produce a product that is useful, which is exactly what many adult chemists do.

What to do

1. Stick two pieces of paper together using just water. What happens when the water evaporates?

2. Place a few spoonfuls of cornstarch in a bowl. Add enough water to make a paste. Use this paste to stick two pieces of paper together. What happens when the paste dries?

3. Follow the same procedure using flour and water. What happens when the paste dries?

4. Give the children a wide assortment of paper to use to make collages or paper constructions. Let them decide which is the best paste to use.

Want to do more?

Make a mixture of cornstarch and water in a clear plastic container and a mixture of flour and water in another container. Place them where they will not be disturbed. Within 15 minutes the cornstarch and water will separate. The flour and water will not change. Make "Magic Matter" in MUDPIES TO MAGNETS from cornstarch and water.

FLOATING RAINBOWS

Language with science

color names
sink
float
layer
mix
separate
bubble

Things you will need

food coloring

large glass jar with water almost to the top

a layer of cooking oil floating on the top 1-2 cm thick — the thicker the oil layer the longer it takes for the coloring to reach the water

Water and food coloring mix, oil and food coloring do not. Food coloring is more dense than oil and doesn't mix with it. Instead, it passes through the oil to mix with the water. The drops of coloring will float in the oil for a moment. When the food coloring finally sinks to the bottom of the oil, it looks like a colored bubble springing a leak as the color escapes into the water. What a surprise! The children can help after the experiment is over by siphoning out the water so you can use the oil again. See **Hodge Podge** for directions for making a siphon.

What to do

1. Place the jar of water and oil on a low stool or box so that as the children watch, it is slightly above their eye level. They may enjoy lying on the floor to watch what happens. Squeeze a few drops of coloring onto the oil.

2. Very slowly the bubbles of coloring will ease through the oil, explode into tiny circles, and float to the bottom of the jar. The colors gradually blend into each other.

NOTE: As with most activities, it is a good idea to try this yourself first so you know how much time to allow for the colors to sink and "explode."

Want to do more?

This is very relaxing and really fascinating to watch. Children can try this for themselves later with smaller jars, and experiment with the amounts of color they use and the combinations of colors they can create. Vary the temperature of the water you use. It does make a difference. See "Rainbow in a Jar" from MUDPIES TO MAGNETS.

MAKE YOUR OWN PERFUME

Language with science

perfume
odor
smell
extract
take out
liquid
gas
pleasant
unpleasant
scent

Things you will need

hammer
wax paper
slices of onions
radishes
limes
lemons
apples
pepper
fresh herbs
mint leaves, etc.

cottage cheese
containers

water

Children enjoy playing scientist with all the mixing, the big words, and the special props. They also enjoy using their senses and making their own special "formulas." MAKE YOUR OWN PERFUME teaches them how to extract odors from plant material. Once they know how, they can do it as often as they like by themselves.

What to do

1. Crush food items with a hammer on pieces of wax paper. Place crushed food items into containers, including any residue on wax paper. Add water to barely cover. Let sit overnight.

2. Pour off clear juice into additional containers. Let the children smell the containers. See if they can identify the odor of the water and match it to a picture or the actual food item from which the odor was extracted.

3. Make the materials available in the room so the children can experiment with making their own perfume. They can also bring in their own materials from home.

Want to do more?

Make smell jars from your perfumes so the children can play a matching game. This is a one day at a time activity as the scents won't last long.

ONLY THE NOSE KNOWS

Language with science

gas
liquid
smell
scent
odor
diffusion
hide
hidden
find
seek
discover

Things you will need

cotton balls

inexpensive cologne

oil of wintergreen

oil of cloves or other strong scent

This activity is a new version of hide and seek. Instead of their eyes, the children use their noses. The children won't really understand how smells travel, but they will certainly find out that they do.

What to do

1. Saturate a cotton ball with a scent. Hide four cotton balls — one that smells and three that do not.

2. Ask the children to find the hidden smell. Explain that they will not find it by seeing — they must use their noses.

3. When the odor source is found, talk about it. How did they detect the smell? Did they see it move? It travels in particles too small for our eyes to see. Explain that the liquid traveled in the form of gas to their noses.

Want to do more?

Try this game outside. How is it different.? Make a list of the children's favorite smells. Experiment with different odors to discover if some travel faster than others. Put out four different smells without hiding them. Let the children walk around the classroom. As they walk the odors will mix. The time will come when they cannot distinguish the different odors. The air will become saturated with the smell of the four odors and their smellers will become numb.

THE AUTOMATIC BALLOON BLOWER UPPER

3

Language with science

reaction
mix
solid
liquid
gas
expand
inflate
bubble

Things you will need

vinegar
baking soda
balloon

clear-plastic bottle with a small opening (i.e., liquid detergent bottle, syrup bottle)

funnel

Technology is the application of science to create an item useful to society. If you have ever watched a young child try to blow up a balloon, you will realize how exciting this technology can be. While vinegar and baking soda won't replace an air pump or good, hard blowing, it's much more fun.

NOTE: Because of the risk of choking, balloons should not be used with young children without direct supervision.

What to do

1. Tell the children that you know how to blow up a balloon without blowing at all. You're going to show them how, then they can try it themselves.

2. Place the end of the balloon around the neck of the funnel. Put about a tablespoon of baking soda in the funnel and shake it gently into the balloon. Remove the funnel and place it in the bottle. Pour about an inch of vinegar into the bottle. Remove the funnel. The amount of soda and vinegar needed varies with the size of the bottle and the balloon. (Try it out before you show the children!) Place the end of the balloon around the neck of the bottle, being careful not to spill the baking soda. When the balloon is attached, gently raise the balloon upright and let the baking soda fall into the bottle. Mixing the baking soda and vinegar causes a chemical reaction — foaming and bubbling — which produces a gas called carbon dioxide (CO_2). That gas is released when the bubbles pop and gets trapped in the balloon and fills it up.

3. Do the experiment several times so the children can see how to do it and that the same thing happens every time. While young children are not going to understand the chemistry of this activity, they will begin to grasp a concept that is basic to science. The concept is that there are things in our world that work in very predictable ways. Every time you mix vinegar and baking soda the same thing happens. The same thing will happen if you do it at home, if you do it again next week; it always happens.

4. Place the materials in the room for two or three children to use at a time. This is a good experiment to do with a partner since attaching the balloon to the bottle is a bit tricky. Some children will need adult help.

Want to do more?

Make your own sequence picture cards following each step of the experiment. Telling another person how to make a BALLOON BLOWER UPPER is a meaningful exercise in sequential memory. Experiment with different bottles and balloons. Add food coloring to the vinegar to make colored foam. Make colored foam in a flat dish and gently touch it with white paper to make a print.

PLAYDOUGH:
A NEW APPROACH

Language with science

dough
soft
wet
dry
sticky
oily
liquid
solid
mix
blend
recipe
experiment

Things you will need

flour
water
salt
vegetable oil

measuring cups and spoons

mixing bowl and spoon

Although most laboratory chemicals are off limits to children, the kitchen holds a wealth of substances ready for experimentation. Using flour, water, salt, and oil, children can pretend to be chemists and experiment to develop a product, playdough, that is just perfect for them. The children begin with an original recipe and then are encouraged to experiment on their own. The final outcome of this activity is a product that the children can make by themselves and play with for days. So put on the lab coats, get the chemicals, and create.

What to do

1. Copy the following recipe for playdough on a large piece of paper or posterboard (see illustration).

250 ml (1 cup) flour

85 ml (1/3 cup) water

85 ml (1/3 cup) salt

15ml (1 Tbsp.) vegetable oil

2. Make playdough. Read the recipe with the children and have them check to see that all the ingredients are ready. Mix up the dough, chatting with them as you work. You can talk about dry and wet ingredients. Let them put their hands in the bowl to mix the flour and salt, and talk about how you can feel the difference between flour and salt even when they are mixed together and you have your eyes closed. Talk about the changes that happen when you add the liquids. Encourage the children to think of words that describe how the dough feels and looks. Make an ample amount for your group and put it out for the children to use. It is a good idea to make a large quantity ahead of time so several children can begin playing right

away. It will keep for at least a week stored in an airtight container, longer if refrigerated.

3. Set up an area for children to make their own playdough. A small table to accommodate 2 or 3 children seems to work best. The children can then talk with each other, compare results, experiment, and really work together. The teacher can be involved or not, as needed. If the ingredients are set out in easy to manage containers, most children can work independently. A dispenser for oil will help control the amount used. Try a small liquid detergent bottle or a liquid hand soap pump dispenser. You will also need a small pitcher for water and a container for the flour. The bag is too hard to use. Give the children pie pans or small plastic bowls for mixing the dough. This will help control the amount they make. They may want to start mixing with spoons, but will probably switch to using their hands.

1 CUP FLOUR

⅓ CUP SALT

⅓ CUP WATER

1 T. VEG. OIL

4. Talk about the fact that you have made playdough using one recipe, but that there are a lot of other recipes. The way to make a new recipe is to experiment and find out what works and that's what they can do. Explain that some things we try work well and others don't. Sometimes you can fix the things that don't work out. Sometimes experiments surprise you. It's fun to try to make playdough that is just right for you. The nice thing about experimenting with playdough is that virtually any combination they use can be made into a usable dough by adding a little more of something. If someone does come up with something beyond salvaging, it's quick and easy to begin again. Urge the children to help each other. When a child comes to you for help, try saying, "Why don't you show it to Sam and see if he has an idea to try." Encourage them to think for themselves. "What don't you like about it? Too crumbly? Well, what could make it stick together better? Why don't you try that and see if it helps." Remember, one goal of this activity is to help children experience the satisfaction that comes from being able to say, "I made it myself."

Want to do more?

Experiment with adding food coloring or powdered tempera paint. Kool-Aid powder creates both color and scent. Try other ingredients. Some recipes substitute liquid dish soap for oil. Oatmeal adds interesting texture. Sugar and salt look alike. Do they both work to make playdough? There are many early childhood books which contain playdough recipes. Make different kinds and let the children compare them. Write down the recipes the children create. Prepare pie or cookie dough and let the children make something they can eat.

GOURMET SCIENCE

Some liquids can mix with each other and some cannot. What better way to find this out than to make your own oil and vinegar salad dressing. Then make a big salad and have a feast.

What to do

1. Give the children containers with water, vinegar, and oil in them. Observe, smell, taste, touch, look at the 3 liquids. What words can they think of to describe these liquids? Make a list. One way chemists describe liquids is to tell what happens when they are mixed together. If they mix together and stay together they are soluble. If they stay separate, they are insoluble.

2. Give the children 3 containers, each filled 1/2 full with the 3 liquids. Add a tablespoon or so of water to each container and stir. Watch what happens. The water and vinegar will mix (they are soluble in each other). So will the water and water. The oil and water will not. Look at the oil and water. The oil will float on top because it is lighter.

3. Now repeat the experiment, adding vinegar to each of the containers. Vinegar and water will be soluble, oil and vinegar will not. Which is lighter or floats, oil or vinegar?

4. Make a simple oil and vinegar dressing. Add some pepper and some herbs. Mix well. Watch as the oil and vinegar separate. Where do the seasonings go?

5. Prepare a salad for a snack so the children can taste the dressing.

Want to do more?

Use small containers to package the basic dressing. Let the children add their own seasonings. The children can make their own labels with catchy names such as "Michael's Super Secret Dressing." They could even list the ingredients. Adults can help, as needed, with the writing. The salad dressing can then be taken home to share with the family.

CRAYON COOKIES

Language with science

melt
solid
liquid
change
hot
cool

Things you will need

crayon pieces
muffin tins

electric skillet or
other heat source

Understanding change is a big part of science. For young children to participate, change needs to be easily recognizable and part of their life experience. In this activity, melting is introduced with a common experience, making crayon "cookies."

What to do

1. With the children's help, peel your collection of old crayons. You can sort them by color if you want solid color cookies. Mix them up if you want multicolored ones. Fill each compartment of the muffin tin with the broken crayons.

2. Place the muffin tin in the electric skillet. Add water to come about halfway up the tin. Turn on medium heat and wait for the crayons to melt. This will take 10-15 minutes. While you're waiting, see how many things you can think of that melt — butter for popcorn, popsicles, ice, chocolate, cheese on cheeseburgers... Be sure to make periodic progress checks. It is important to see that melting is a gradual process.

NOTE: Obviously, heat can be dangerous with young children. Take the appropriate precautions!

3. When the crayons are completely melted, remove the muffin tin from the skillet. Let the children see what is happening as the crayons "unmelt." The cookies will solidify faster if you put the tin in a cake pan half filled with ice water. This is a good time for singing or some other activity, again with periodic progress checks.

4. What next? Use them, of course!

Want to do more?

Melt some of the things the children mentioned. Cool the materials by placing in freezer. How many return to original consistency? How do we use melted foods in our homes or restaurants? Some things that melt "weirdly" are sugar, chocolate, mayonnaise. What things can they think of that don't melt? Try them and see if the predictions are correct. Does melted Jell-O taste different than solid Jell-O? Melt a popsicle and refreeze in a new shape. Does it taste the same in both shapes?

CRYSTAL FLOWER GARDEN

3+

Language with science

crystals
grow
salt
ammonia
mixture
solution
chemicals

Things you will need

cotton swabs cut in half

pipe cleaners cut in 5 cm (2 in) pieces

pieces of oil based clay

food coloring
water
liquid bluing
salt
ammonia

flat dishes — plastic margarine tubs work well (salt will corrode a metal dish)

This approach to growing crystals allows for some creative involvement. You can make beautiful and varied flower-like formations by using pipe cleaner designs and cotton swabs for the crystals to climb. Through repeating the activity several times, children will discover ways to arrange the materials to create their own special effects. Each child can grow a unique little crystal garden.

What to do
Teacher:

1. Make up a solution of:

   125 ml (1/2 cup) water

   60 ml (4 T) liquid bluing

   60 ml (4 T) salt

   20 ml (4 t) ammonia (add last)

2. Soak ends of Q-tips in food coloring the day before and allow to dry. Put drops of food coloring on the pipe cleaners.

Children:

1. Place a lump of clay on the bottom of the dish. Push 2-4 cotton swabs and/or pipe cleaners into the clay.

2. Pour the crystal flower solution in the cup so the clay and the first centimeter (1/2 in.) of the cotton swabs are covered.

3. Set the dish in an open space where it will not be bumped much and watch your flowers grow. Crystals will begin to form within a few hours unless it is very humid.

Want to do more?
Use the same solution poured over charcoal, rocks, sponges, or bricks. Place one in a warm place and one in a cold place. Try it in the refrigerator. Does it grow faster, slower, or at the same rate as the one outside? Look at the crystals with a magnifier. Compare with natural crystals or other crystals you have grown. Arrange the pipe cleaners or other items and predict what the formation will look like.

HOW TO MAKE A FLOATER SINK

Language with science

surface
tension
middle
center
side

Things you will need

water

pepper

small aluminum pie tin

tongue depressor or spoon for stirring

liquid soap

Water is a wonderful substance. It has qualities that make it the most important liquid on earth. One of those qualities is that water has a high surface tension. This means that the molecules hug to each other and form a surface that is not easily penetrated. Thus, objects can lay on water and be supported by the surface. Some substances break that tension so that water can do work for us. One of those surface tension breakers is soap. Let's see what soap does. While we're at it, this is a fun way to use the words middle, center, and side.

What to do

1. Fill the pie tin about half full of water. Gently sprinkle the pepper on top of the water. What can be keeping the pepper on top of the water? It's surface tension. The molecules are so close together that the pepper can't go through.

2. Dribble a drop of the liquid soap down the SIDE of the pan. What happens? Like magic, the pepper sinks.

3. Start again with a well rinsed pan. This time place a drop in the MIDDLE or CENTER of the pan. Encourage the children to describe what they see. The pepper sinks in a very different pattern.

4. As the children talk about what is happening, use the words middle, center, and side to compare what they've done. For young children who are just becoming familiar with these words, this activity

provides concrete experience in their use. Use the words naturally. A heavy emphasis can quickly change a happy time of messing about with science into a dull vocabulary lesson. Repeated use in context will eventually get the point across and in a more meaningful way.

Want to do more?

Have the children perform the experiment with solid soap rather than liquid detergent. Have children again add pepper and water to the pie tin. Stir it. Do the pepper and water mix? What happens when you stop stirring? Stirring is another way to break the surface tension and make the pepper sink.

BAKING SODA + VINEGAR = BUBBLES

Language with science

reaction
chemicals

sodium bicar-
bonate

base
acid
acetic acid
vinegar
mix
foam
bubble

Things you will need

for each group —
a squeeze bottle
of vinegar (i.e.,
small liquid deter-
gent bottle)

a bowl of baking
soda

small spoons
small cups

Chemical reactions occur when two chemicals unite or react to form a compound that is unlike the original substances and cannot be changed back to its original form. Chemical reactions are often accompanied by some sort of visible reaction. So what does all this have to do with young children? First, it's lots of fun to mix two everyday ingredients and have such exciting results. Second, it happens every time! One important concept the children can begin to grasp is that some things are predictable. Vinegar (acetic acid) and baking soda (sodium bicarbonate) create lots of bubbles no matter who does the mixing. This is an experiment the children can do as often as they like and the same thing will always happen. That concept is a big part of science.

What to do

1. Place the materials on the table in front of the children and ask the children to drop a spoonful of the white powder in their cups. Ask them to squirt a little of the liquid onto the white powder.

2. Watch as the first child squirts in the vinegar. The others will want to follow quickly. After everyone has a chance, talk about what happened. What was the same about everyone's experiment? Why were there differences? Could it be how much vinegar was squirted or could it be how the powder was spread across the cup? Other ideas?

3. Have them wash out their cups and try this time to see if they can find a way to get the most bubbles. What's the secret? Does it help to put vinegar in first and the powder on top? Sprinkle the powder in slowly or drop the vinegar slowly? What do they think works best?

4. As you and the children talk while they're working, share the words sodium bicarbonate and acetic acid. Just as many children enjoy wrapping their tongues around dinosaur names, many will enjoy trying out the words chemists use. Share "chemical reaction" with them in the same

informal way. You may want to write the words, along with vinegar and baking soda. Some children will enjoy looking at them, comparing them, and perhaps finding them on the original containers.

5. Keep the materials readily available so that children can continue to explore independently.

Want to do more?

Try the experiment with baking soda and lemon juice. Try using other white powders. What happens? See "The Automatic Balloon Blower Upper" in this chapter. Try "The Dunking Raisins" in MUDPIES TO MAGNETS.

NOTE: For those of you who want to know, this is a typical chemical reaction in which an acid — vinegar, reacts with a base — baking soda, to produce a new chemical — a salt. The bubbles that form are full of carbon dioxide, a gas that is released in the process.

RUST:
A CLOSER LOOK

4

Language with science

rust
chemical change
rusting
steel or iron
water

Things you will need

2 Ziploc bags

steel wool (cut into 2 cm x 2 cm pieces)

collection of rusty objects

timer

One of the most common chemical reactions around us is the oxidizing of iron and steel metals. In this reaction, the iron forms a new compound by uniting with oxygen. That new compound is called iron oxide or rust. The action is enhanced by water. Because the rusting occurs so quickly in steel wool, it is easy to see the cause and effect relationship. Let's try.

NOTE: If you bring this experiment to young children out of the blue, it will probably be of little value. If, however, it is done following the discovery of rusty toys in the sandbox, it may help them think about a meaningful question.

What to do

1. Explain that a chemical change that occurs often in the environment is rusting. Has anyone seen something rusty? Share the rusty objects in your collection with the children.

2. What makes things rust? Any ideas? Talk about any ideas they may have, and if possible, try them. How else do you find out if your guess is right or wrong? Wrong? So what! Just try something else. Here is an experiment.

3. Put a piece of steel wool in one of the bags and seal it. Put wet steel wool in the other bag and seal it.

4. Set the timer and return every 30 minutes to watch what happens. Each time you check the bags, encourage the children to talk about the changes they see. Write down their descriptions.

5. Watch until rust has completely covered the steel wool. What does the other piece of steel wool look like? Why do you suppose it still looks the same?

Want to do more?

Take pictures or have the children draw pictures of the steel wool every 30 minutes. Make your own sequence cards. Collect metal objects and put them in wet baggies. See which things rust. Classify rusting metals with a magnet, only those with magnetic properties rust. Can you stop rusting? Coat something that rusts with oil and see what happens.

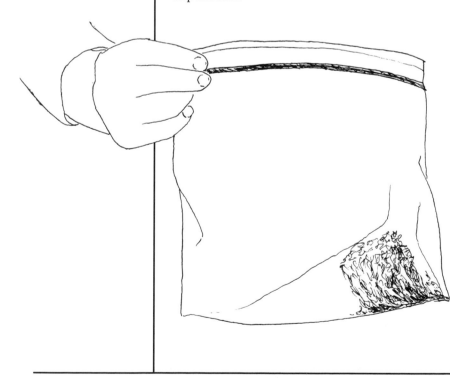

NOW YOU SEE IT, NOW YOU DON'T

Language with science

dissolve
stir
mix
solution
clear
soluble
insoluble
settle
sediment
disappear

Things you will need

clear plastic cups
sugar cubes
cornstarch
spoons
water

mixing powders
such as:
  salt
  pepper
  baking soda
  powdered
    sugar
  brown sugar
  cinnamon
  flour
  baking powder
  baby powder
  and soap
    powder

This activity begins with a simple group introduction to the concept of dissolving substances in water to make a solution. From that point on, the children are in charge. With a simple "kitchen" laboratory, they will find out all sorts of things about solutions and mixtures, and probably a good many other things as well. Let them experiment!

What to do

1. Give each child a cup of water, a sugar cube, and a spoon. Taste the sugar cube. How does it taste? What does it feel like when you lick it with your tongue? What does it look like?

2. Put the sugar cubes in the water. What happens? How do the children describe what they see? Stir the sugar and water. Where did the sugar go? Encourage the children to speculate freely. What do they think happened?

3. Is the sugar still there? How can we find out? Taste the water. Does the sugar taste the same? Does it feel the same? The sugar dissolved in the water. It disappeared from our eyes, but not from our tongues! Dissolving changes some things about sugar, but not everything.

4. Show them the cornstarch. This is white and powdery like sugar. Maybe it will dissolve, too. Try it. Does the same thing happen? Yes, it mixes, but what happens when you stop stirring? Cornstarch is insoluble in water and will settle to the bottom after a time. This settled material is called sediment.

5. Set up a solutions table in the room. Include several substances such as salt, pepper, baking soda, powdered sugar, brown sugar, cinnamon, flour, baking powder, baby powder, and soap powder. Remind the children about tasting safety. (These powders are for mixing, not tasting. You only taste things when you know what they are and an adult says it's okay.) Let the children experiment with mixing the powders with water. Small containers such as medicine cups will control the amounts

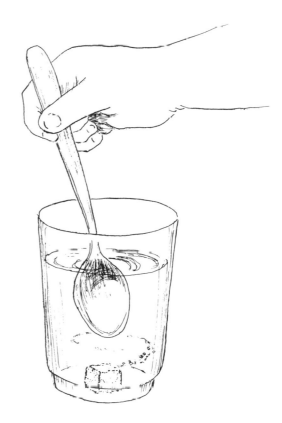

mixed. Informal conversation with the children can encourage them to describe what they see and what they expect to happen. It won't take long for them to know and remember which powders dissolve and which don't. More importantly, it won't take them long to become absorbed in a very intriguing experience. (Don't forget to tell them that chemists clean their equipment when they finish an experiment.)

Want to do more?

Leave a glass of each solution to evaporate. See what happens. Add other liquids such as vegetable oil, white vinegar, and cider vinegar. Does water colored blue with food coloring bring the same results? See "Muddy, Muddy River" in the **Earth Explorations** chapter, the crystal growing activities listed in the table of contents, and "Grow a Rock" in MUDPIES TO MAGNETS.

KOOL-AID CHEMISTRY

Language with science

solution
dilution
strong
weak
dissolve
stir
taste
mix
dark
light

Things you will need

powdered drink mixture — a presweetened one simplifies the task

measuring spoons

clear drinking glasses

water
spoons or stirrers

When children drink Kool-Aid, the last thing that they think of is chemistry. What they consider is taste. Is it too sweet? Is it too watery? Or is it just right? By making their own Kool-Aid, children can use sight and taste to compare the dilution of mixtures. They become chemists as they explore methods for determining the solution to dilution.

What to do

1. Give each child a glass half full of water and a spoon for stirring.

2. Give each child or group of children a measuring spoon. Some will have a 1/4 teaspoon, some a tablespoon, and so on.

3. Ask the children to place 1 spoonful of the drink mixture into their glasses. Stir until all is dissolved.

4. Have the students compare the way their drink looks with others in the group. Compare color. Whose is the darkest? Whose is the lightest? Are there some that are about the same? How do they guess their Kool-Aid will taste? Too strong? Too weak? Just right? Taste and find out.

5. What do they think is the best amount of drink mix to use? Read the label on the can. Do the children agree or disagree with the directions?

6. Add more water or more Kool-Aid so each child can enjoy a tasty drink.

Want to do more?

Order the dilutions from strongest to weakest. Place the words strongest and weakest next to the appropriate containers. Try lemonade so the color is not as obvious. Use cuisinaire rods to compare the amount of mixture put in each cup. Use a ones rod to equal 1/4 teaspoon.

HOW DENSE IS DENSITY?

Language with science

graph
float
sink
dense
lighter
heavier
more
less
layer

Things you will need

1 gallon glass jar
water
cooking oil
molasses
cork
apple slice
paper clip
grape
piece of candle

small rubber eraser

spoon
pencil
paper

Sink and float are two commonly taught school activities. They are easy to set up, and show cause and effect through simple manipulation. Most sink and float activities involve water. What we are really dealing with in sink or float is the density of objects. Density refers to the number of molecules packed into a given area. When objects have many molecules packed together and are heavier than water, they sink. The opposite is true of objects lighter than water — they float.

So what about liquids? Well, liquids are a little different because you have another variable — solubility. Liquids that can't mix with water are either heavier or lighter than water. Most petroleum products are lighter and float. Some liquids such as molasses will mix with water, but do so very slowly. Molasses will sink unless it is stirred. Other liquids such as alcohol mix with water easily. Although they may be heavier or lighter, the difference is harder to detect. Try this sink and float activity and discover some facts for yourselves.

OIL

WATER

MOLASSES

What to do

1. Pour the liquids into the glass container one at a time. Pour the liquids over a spoon so they do not mix.

2. Observe how the liquids separate into three different layers.

3. What liquid sinks to the bottom? Which one is in the middle? Which liquid is on top? Which is the heaviest, lightest? Which has the greatest density? Least density?

4. Take turns putting things in the jar. Talk about what you see. Can you find something that floats in water but sinks in oil? How about something that sinks in water but floats in molasses? Can you find a way to keep a record of your observations?

Want to do more?

Make an "Ocean in a Jar" in MUDPIES TO MAGNETS. Try other liquids. Keep an eye on the jar for awhile. What eventually happens to the molasses?

HOW FAST DOES YOUR CRYSTAL GROW

Language with science

crystals
igneous
rocks
sparkling
hard
soft
evaporate

Things you will need

four 2 cm (1 inch) square cubes cut from rubber sponge

ammonia
salt
water
liquid bluing

pie pan (glass or aluminum)

measuring cup
spoon

Crystals are found in igneous rocks. When children see these rocks with their crystals exposed, they are fascinated by their sparkling beauty. This activity demonstrates one way in which crystals can be grown. They form as water evaporates from the solution saturated materials that are provided below. With a little care, children can grown huge formations of crystals.

What to do

1. Place 2 cm (1 inch) square cubes of rubber sponge in the pie pan.

2. Pour the following materials in amounts designated into the pie pan.

   60 ml water (1/4 cup)

   60 ml table salt (4 tablespoons)

   60 ml bluing (4 tablespoons)

   16 ml ammonia (1 tablespoon)

3. Stir and spoon the mixture over the sponges until they are thoroughly soaked.

4. Place the pie pan on a table near a window.

5. Have the children make observations of the mixture every 2 hours. The crystalization begins immediately; however, it is most noticeable after an overnight soak. Then the crystals will grow continuously like plants with the look of coral. By adding small amounts of water on the third day, this phenomenon of crystalization can be observed for a week or longer.

Want to do more?

Crystals can be grown from such common substances as salt or alum. Mix water with these substances and compare the crystal growth to each other. Put in a cold, dry place, crystals grow bigger. The lower the evaporation, the bigger the crystals. Copper sulfate also grows interesting crystals but is poisonous, so supervise its use carefully.

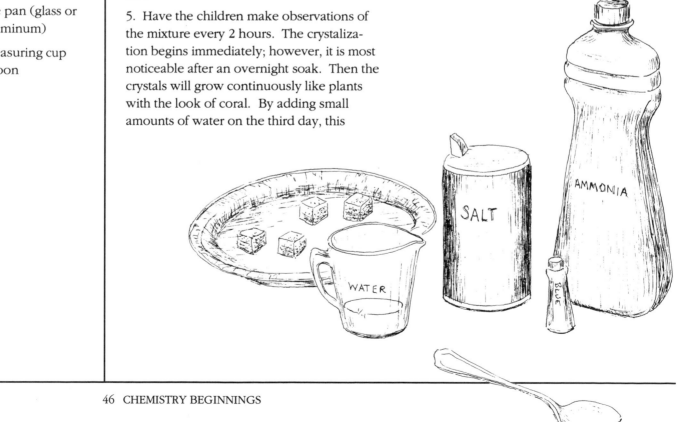

COLORED WATER CHEMISTRY

Right in front of their eyes blue and yellow mix and create green. Is it magic? It may seem to be, but it's not. It is something each child can control and do over and over until it's not magic because "I can do it."

Language with science

solutions
combination
primary colors
mix
secondary colors
mixture
experiment

Things you will need

small clear containers

large dish pan

clear squeeze bottles such as detergent or syrup bottles — 3 for each set-up

red, yellow and blue food coloring

What to do

1. Each set-up should include one bottle each of red, yellow, and blue colored water, several clear containers for mixing, and a dish pan or bucket to pour water into when the child is finished.

2. Introduce the materials and tell the children that they are color chemists. They can combine the water in different ways to make colored solutions. They can experiment with different mixtures to find ways to make their favorite colors. You can use the words primary colors and secondary colors and color names as you talk with the children about their work. You don't need to make an issue of it. Having fun making colors is the important thing.

3. After the children have had plenty of time to experiment independently, pose some questions: What if you use a little red and a lot of yellow, will you still make orange? How many different colors can you make that have red in them? How many shades of purple can you make?

Want to do more?

Make a rainbow of cups of colored water. Prepare "formula cards"

$$B + Y = G$$

$$B + R = V$$

$$Y + R = O$$

$$B + Y + R = YUK$$

Show these cards and have the young chemists create the mixtures. Fill a lot of 2 liter bottles with the primary colors and have an outdoor rainbow making festival. Tape the caps on a few of the bottles. Very young children enjoy carting around color bottles. You know how much they enjoy playing with big, heavy things. See "Egg Carton Rainbows" in MUDPIES TO MAGNETS.

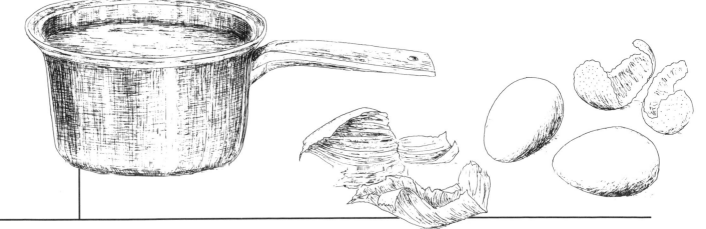

BRRRRR — IT'S COLD

Language with science

freeze
frozen
crystallize
liquids
predict
expand
expansion
temperature
cold
warm
room temperature
freezer
before
after
cryogenics

Things you will need

plastic film
canisters with lids
(the clear ones
are best)

various
household
liquids
    water
    milk
    liquid detergent
    cooking oil
    catsup
    honey
    mustard

Jell-o
small box lined
with foil

freezer

Cryogenics is the study of the effects of extreme cold on substances. The extent of the average child's knowledge of this subject can be worded succinctly: Put water in the freezer and it makes an ice cube! Many children who have ice makers don't even realize that water is needed. Ice cubes just appear. This activity explores what happens to different types of liquids when they are chilled to the point of freezing. It also provides an effective way to use the words BEFORE and AFTER. What did the honey look like BEFORE we put it in the freezer? What did it look like AFTER we put it in the freezer? Be honest — do you know what frozen honey looks like? You don't care?! Well, maybe you'll like the frozen Jell-O pops better.

What to do

1. Talk with children about what happens when water is frozen. Show examples using ice cubes. Can they think of some other frozen things? Do all liquids react the same way? Have the children fill the film canisters with a variety of liquids. Put on the lids. Assist them by labeling each canister with its content. Put the canisters in the box and place in a freezer overnight.

2. Have the children predict what will happen to the liquids. Will it freeze? What will it look like? Write down their predictions.

3. The next day remove the box and examine the canisters. Observe and discuss the changes that have taken place. Some canisters will have no lids because of expansion, some will have contents that have crystallized and are not completely solid. What happens to these liquids? Why don't they all do the same thing when frozen?

4. Now for your treat. Pour Jell-O into an ice cube tray to freeze your own Jell-O pops. While they're freezing ask the children to think of words to describe regular Jell-O. Can they make their bodies move the way Jell-O moves? While eating the Jell-O pops, go through the same process about frozen Jell-O.

Want to do more?

Discuss what happens to foods that are frozen. Why don't they spoil? What happens to the frozen liquids when they melt? Are they the SAME or DIFFERENT than the liquid that hasn't been frozen? In cold weather, find frozen puddles and put things outside to freeze. Add lots of food coloring to ice cubes and use them to color on coffee filters or other absorbent paper. See "Tin Can Ice Cream" in HUG A TREE.

SOLUTION OF THE DAY

Language with science

mix
solution
day

Things you will need

bowls
cups
spoons
scoops
soap powder
sugar
milk
water
lemonade
chocolate
powdered milk
vinegar
cucumbers

Following directions, instructions, and recipes are all techniques that scientists use to conduct their research. In SOLUTION OF THE DAY, the children follow a picture recipe to create a different solution for each day of the week.

What to do

1. Develop a chart for the week with the materials needed to prepare the solutions used for each day (see illustration).

2. Talk about what a solution is and how it is made. Most solutions are either food or are used to do work for us.

3. Place all the materials at the science center table.

4. Place the recipe chart out for children to use. Individually or in small groups, have them prepare the recipe for the solution of the day.

Want to do more?

Add another week of solutions from our list above or create some of your own.

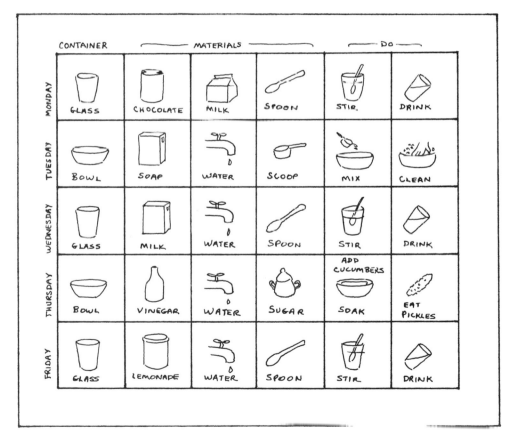

HOW THINGS WORK:
FIRST PHYSICS

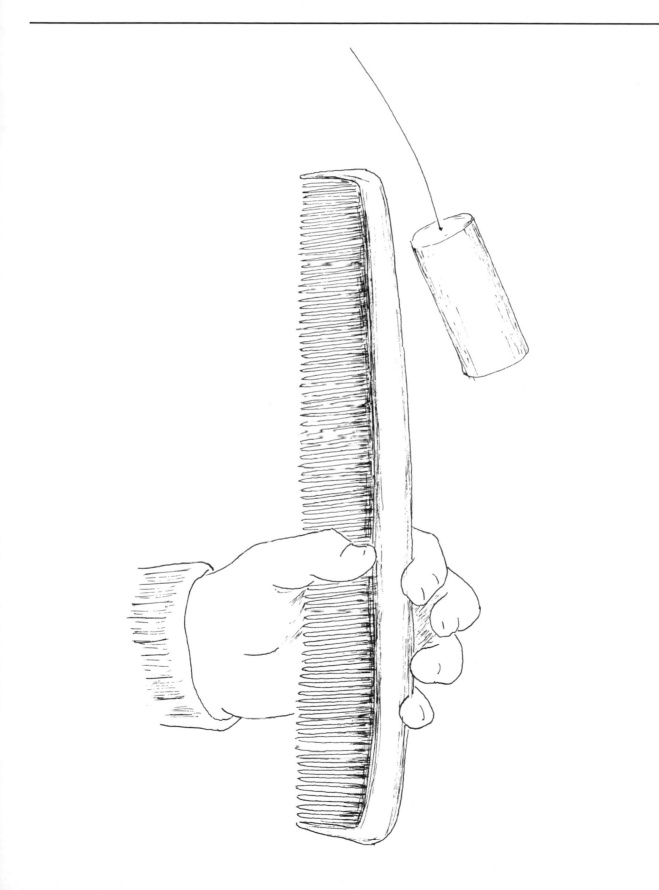

HOW THINGS WORK: FIRST PHYSICS

Physics is

- the study of matter and energy and their relationship to each other. Matter is anything that occupies space, while energy refers to the ability to do work. Physics is concerned with atoms, subatomic particles, molecules, solids, liquids, gases, and describes these in terms of their mass and density.
- a discipline that can be used by all disciplines because it deals with the basic forces that affect all matter. When energy is studied, the emphasis is placed on work, and work implies motion. Physics is the source of information for all forms of energy, including nuclear energy
- studied by physicists, and they work hard to help us understand about the physical properties of matter and energy.

Ideas to share with children

- A complex study of space by astrophysicists is attempting to tell how old the cosmos is and of what it is composed. That may help us understand the forces affecting Earth.
- Physicists have developed machines in hospitals that can look inside the human body to tell what is right and what is wrong when we are sick or hurt. The X-ray machine is one example of such a machine. Dentists and doctors both use it.
- All the computer inner workings were and are being designed by physicists who are working to make computers smaller and more powerful.
- Energy sources create power that is sent over lines or through the air. Physicists study how to send that energy, how to use it, and are looking for ways to conserve and create new energy forms. Nuclear energy was, to a large degree, created by physicists.
- When a rocket goes up or a vehicle stops fast in an emergency, then physics gives us knowledge of that happening by placing it in its basic form. Mathematics is the tool of the physicist in studying matter and energy; and the biggest tool used for processing the information is the computer. Future physicists must learn mathematics and must know how to use a computer.

Things to do

- Understanding physics is easy because it explains so many of the basic forces and happenings in our everyday lives. Modern day physics is not as easy to observe because the research is so technical. Every engineer is applying the principles of physics, so inviting one in to talk may be helpful.
- Much of the physicist's equipment is electronic. A physics laboratory and a television laboratory will look much the same. You remember we said they studied energy. Electronics is an application of the use of energy.

- Dressing up like a physicist is not easy because they have no real stereotype. But if you want to, put on a white lab jacket, no safety glasses, and add a few props. Batteries, bulbs, and wires are some. Pendulums, prisms, magnets, lenses, a Slinky to make waves, an inclined plane with marble, and a computer also add to the picture. A slide rule used to be an absolute necessity before the computer.
- Famous physicists include Isaac Newton, Galileo, Marie Curie, Thomas Edison, Sally Ride, Albert Einstein, James Watt, Enrico Fermi. and Susan Wyckoff.
- The following physics ideas can be found in:

HUG A TREE	The Sun Won't Shine Through You
	How Do You Measure Things?
	Fill That Space — An Area Game
	Water Clocks
	Measure Shadows
MUDPIES TO MAGNETS	Dancing Droppers
	The Main Attraction: Magnet Boxes
	Shadow Box
	Cling to Me
	Real Puzzles
	Sound Traveler
	Balancing Toys
	Pulley into Line
	Rampin' It
	Call Me
	Rolling, Rolling, Rolling
	Bags of Energy
	Thunk or Ding
	What's That Sound
	Let There Be Light
	Shadow, Shadow on the Wall
	Magical Magnet Masterpieces
	Pendulum Patterns in the Sand
	Color Makers
	Flashlight Tag

HUMMERS

Language with science

vibrate
sound
blow
kazoo
hum

When we take scientific knowledge that we possess and create a machine that is useful to us for another task, we call this process technology. Thus our knowledge about sound can be used to make this machine, the kazoo. The sound we produce as we hum into a kazoo is caused by the vibration of our own vocal cords. As the sound travels down to the end of the tube, it increases in loudness as the plastic paper begins an additional vibration. All sounds are caused by vibrations, but some sounds are more pleasant than others. We love the sound of music. With our humming and kazoos let's create a song.

Things you will need

toilet paper tubes

aluminum foil tubes or christmas paper tubes

wax paper
rubber bands
paper punch

scissors (cut wax paper in squares large enough to cover the end of the tubes)

What to do

1. Have the children collect and decorate individual kazoo tubes. Don't use water color markers or you'll have rainbow mouths and hands!

2. Have each child select a piece of wax paper and a rubber band.

3. Make a hole in the tube using a paper punch. Adults can help as needed.

4. Place the wax paper in position and add the rubber band (see drawing).

5. Practice humming. This is hard for some children to grasp at first. Humming can be made louder by using a machine called a kazoo. When we hum a noise is made in our throat. The sound can be passed to the kazoo through the air. You may have a few children who never quite manage to hum. They'll still have a good time tootling with their instruments.

Want to do more?

Form a kazoo band. Try different kazoo lenths. What other instruments can you make?

DRUM IN A JAR

Language with science

vibrations
sound
drum
rhythm

Things you will need

pint or quart jar with two part lid, the type used for canning

This activity uses some very common household items to construct an instrument. It takes the simple idea of vibrating sound through a drum-like shape, but throws in the variability of water sloshing against the lid and constantly changing the amount of space available to vibrate and expand the sound. The only problem with the instrument is its breakability, so drum with care or the noise won't be there.

What to do

1. Fill the jar half full of water. Close the lid tightly. Hold the container in your hand, leaving both ends free.

2. Tip the container so the water waves in the jar.

3. Hit the glass end of the jar with the fingers of your other hand. You should hear fine drumming sounds.

4. How many different sounds and rhythms can you create?

Want to do more?

Add mineral oil. See "Ocean in a Jar" in MUDPIES TO MAGNETS. Try different lids. Change the level of water in the jar. Add food coloring to the jar to make a rainbow of drums. Experiment with jars of different shapes and sizes.

DANCE AROUND THE WATER

Language with science

water
float
sink
sunk
wet
dry
chart
same
different

Things you will need

open area

tub of water

2 sheets of large paper

masking tape

towel

collection of objects (appropriate size for tub), such as:

    spoon
    sponge
    paper
    small car
    blocks
    crayon
    scissors
    puzzle piece
    kleenex tissue
    cup (results will depend on angle of placement in the water)

The very youngest two's and three's are anxious to have "hands-on" activities and yet keep moving all the while. This little experiment with water will meet both those needs. The children will gather objects, predict results, dance and sing, as well as make a chart.

What to do

1. Prepare charts with a picture of a sinking and floating object. Post at children's eye level, near where you will do your experiment.

2. Help the children collect familiar objects to find out if they sink or float. Some duplicate items are okay, as you can use them together in the same dance, as well as discuss if similar items have the same or different results and why.

3. Put the tub of water, at least three inches deep, on the floor in the center of the the open area. Allow plenty of room for dancing around the tub.

4. Introduce the children to this simple chant:

    Dance around the water

    I brought a (*name of object*) to play

    Does it sink? Does it float?

    Let's put it in and see.

5. Give a child an object (several children, if duplicate items are used). Ask the children to predict if the object will sink or float. The entire group begins to dance and chant as they move around the tub of water. When the chant is over, the children put their object into the tub.

6. Briefly discuss if the object floated on the top of the water or sank to the bottom of the tub.

7. Have a towel ready to dry objects. Allow the children to identify which chart to tape the object on. (This will seem bulky, just tape as well as you can!)

8. Move along quickly and continue to repeat the chant until all the children have a turn to dance with an object and everything is charted.

9. Notice and discuss the results indicated by the charts. Leave the charts posted for a day or so as these youngsters will enjoy recalling the game and even naming the objects. They may also share the charts with a caregiver who picks them up that day.

Want to do more?

Encourage children to try sinking and floating at home in the bath, sink, or pool (with parents' permission, of course). Let them share the results with you another day. Expand your charts to include items the children bring from home. Write their name next to the item on the chart. It will be something they really remember. Find things that both sink and float — cups, pie pans, etc.

Contributed by Sherry Marti, Home Day Care Provider

GOOD VIBRATIONS

Language with science

sound
vibration
friction
noise
paper
cups
produce
water
wet
string

Things you will need

paper cups
nail
paper clips
string
water

Sounds are caused by vibrations. When we strike the string on a guitar, we hear a sound. If a rubber band is stretched over a shoe box and plucked, we also hear a sound. This sound is the result of a movement called a vibration. This activity is a fun way to show children another way that vibration can produce sound. It incorporates friction as the energy source for the vibration. The children will enjoy the weird sounds that they can make as they play their musical cups.

What to do

1. Punch a hole in the base of a paper cup using a sharp object.

2. Insert 30-50 cm length of string into the hole.

3. Tie a paper clip inside the cup and pull into place.

4. Use water to soak the string.

5. Place cup in one hand and firmly place the fingers of your other hand on the wet string, just beneath the base of the cup.

6. Now pull your fingers down the string. What happens? If it doesn't work well, you need more water or more practice. If it does work well, you'll sound like a herd of elephants.

Want to do more?

Use cups of various sizes and compare the sounds that are made. Also experiment with different size string and different kinds of string. Are all the sounds the same?

STORED ENERGY MACHINE

Language with science

machine
energy
roll
forward
backward
return
repeat

Things you will need

dried baby food cans (need extra lids to balance machine)

paper clips
coffee cans
weights
bag ties
rubber bands

This activity explains the story of energy. It is a machine that can take up energy, store it, and use the energy to roll back to the starting point. This machine is not easy for children to make, but will provide hours of fun, especially if you throw in a few that don't work, have heavier rubber bands, or are of varying sizes. What happens inside the machine is that the rubber band is twisted up as it is rolled across the floor, because gravity holds the weight in place, instead of allowing it to turn. When friction stops the can, the energy in the twisted rubber band sends the machine back to its starting point.

What to do

1. Create the stored energy machine (see drawing). Make 6 or more using different rubber bands and different sized cans. Label each can A, B, C or 1, 2, 3, or paint different colors. The labeling will depend on the skill you wish the children to learn.

2. Present these to children and let them play with the machines. Have 1 or 2 without rubber bands or without weights.

3. Tell the children their task as scientists is to determine which is the strongest. How will they tell? They have to measure how far the stored energy machine comes back. Explain how it works, and why some don't work because of the weight on the rubber band.

4. Create an inclined plane. Have the children roll the stored energy machines down the plane from the same spot. When it backs up (returns), compare the distance. Order the machines from best to worst.

Want to do more?

Let those who are able build more machines to test. See if pushing harder makes the machine come back further. Do the different sized rubber bands make a difference? What about different weights?

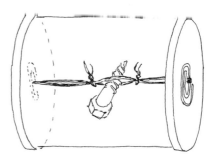

REFLECTION CONNECTION

Language with science

light
objects
visible
illuminate
reflected light
lit
source
see
color names

Things you will need

shoe box with lid

pieces of note cards

small objects (both light and dark colored) to place in box

We see objects because light reflecting from them hits our eyes. When we see red, white, blue, or any of the colors, it is because we have been taught that certain stimuli on our eyes represent that color. Our eyes receive the light, and our brain learns to match the color to the appropriate color name. When no light is present to be reflected into our eyes, we cannot see. Experiment with this and find out for yourself.

What to do

1. Take a shoe box and cut a 5 cm square door in the lower left side. Cut an eye-size peep hole in the front of the box (see drawing).

2. Place an object in the box with the door closed and have a child look through the peep hole. What can you see? With the door closed, nothing, total darkness.

3. Now open the side door. What can you see now? As the door is opened light will be allowed into the box. It will reflect off the object and allow it to be seen.

4. Try dark as well as light colored objects. Talk about how almost everything is seen because of light reflected into our eyes.

Want to do more?

Discuss the safety aspects. Why wear reflective colors at night on our shoes or clothes? Bring in reflective clothing and check this in the reflector box.

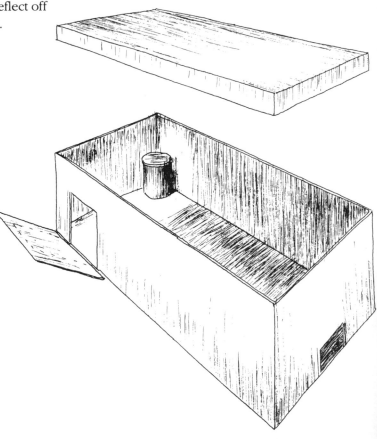

PAINT ROLLER WAVES

Language with science

float
fluids
flow
sink
waves
current

Things you will need

paint rollers
smooth sidewalk
water hose
leaves
sticks
marbles
pencils

pairs of objects
from the classroom

The flow of waves and fluid mechanics is a highly technical knowledge that is studied in wave tanks or through computer based receiving devices. Waves and fluids can, however, be studied by children in a much easier way. One study of fluids that we all remember is floating leaves and sticks down gutter rivers after snow melts or rainstorms. This activity creates the opportunity to observe how the flow of waves effects the movement of objects, without waiting for the next rain.

What to do

1. Set up a sidewalk area by cleaning it with a hose. This area should be fairly large, very flat, smooth, and even.

2. Hook up the hose and flood this area with water. Have the hose on or place a soaker hose over the area so the water flows evenly over a large area.

3. Place the items on the surface along with the paint rollers. Show the children how to use the paint rollers to push water across the surface of the sidewalk.

4. Ask the children to sort the objects into groups by how they move in the "waves" created by the paint rollers.

Want to do more?

Take out "mystery items" and ask the children to predict the results, then prove their predictions by using the roller. Can the children think of ways to help objects move? Do some rollers work better than others? Is there a best way to use the rollers to move objects? See "The Great Air Machine Race" in MUDPIES TO MAGNETS for an activity using air to move objects.

GALILEO'S DROP

Language with science

Galileo
gravity
theory
scientist
object
fall
same
different
speed
fast
slow
sound
hit
first
second

Things you will need

a large ball that can be held in one hand — a soft ball or a foam rubber ball work well

marble

cookie sheet

chair that is safe to stand on

When we run and fall, why do we fall down? When acorns fall from an oak tree, why do they hit the ground? The force that pulls both you and the acorn down to the ground is called gravity. Many years ago, a scientist named Galileo thought that all things are pulled down to the ground at the same speed no matter what they weigh. He tried an experiment to see if he was right or wrong. Try Galileo's experiment yourself. See what he discovered.

What to do

1. The children's interest in this activity depends on the degree to which they are involved in speculating about the outcome and choosing items for experimentation. Tell them briefly about Galileo. Emphasize the fact that he was a man with a question. He knew that when things were dropped they always fell to the ground. He wondered if big, heavy things fell faster than small, light things. He thought of an experiment to try that might answer his question. He decided to try dropping two things at the same time from a high place to see if they would land at the same time or at different times. Show them the marble and the ball. Ask them what they think will happen if you hold them even and drop them at the same time. Will they hit the cookie sheet at the same time, or will one hit it first?

2. Place a cookie sheet on the floor next to the chair. Stand on the chair holding the marble in one hand and the ball in the other hand. Hold your arms as high as you can over the cookie sheet. Listen for the sound of them hitting the cookie sheet. Open both hands at the same time so they start to drop at the same time.

3. Which one lands first? Try it again. What happens? Do the results suprise you? What else do you think we should drop? Let the children find things to drop and try the experiment themselves. They can take turns experimenting during a free choice time.

4. Later, after the children have had time to experiment, ask, "What did you find out?" Have the children make up a rule that tells what happens when things fall. What did Galileo learn? He learned the same thing we did. **Everything falls at the same rate**.

NOTE: A factor which the children may run into is that the shape of an object can change the rate of fall. A feather or a sheet of paper may hit the ground later because it pushes against air, which slows its fall. See **Flight and Space** activities for experiments with air resistance.

Want to do more?

Test objects that are the same size and shape, but different weights. Try dropping two sheets of paper, one flat and one crumpled into a ball. What happens? Let the children invent ways to make things fall slower.

WHO CAN BEAT GRAVITY?

Language with science

gravity
fall
force
up
down

Things you will need

paper
balloons

Gravity is a relentless force that affects everything on earth. It is a continuous force that pulls everything down, down, down. This activity presents a fun way to attempt to beat the force of gravity. By batting balloons and attempting to keep them off the ground, the children eventually discover that it is impossible to win against gravity. That is unless some smart kid remembers outer space. You might tell them they can beat gravity if they become astronauts. If you haven't done any work with the concept of gravity, do "Galileo's Drop" first.

What to do

1. Talk about gravity. Crumple up paper and show how it falls to the ground, to the floor, to the top of the table. It falls until an object stops it. Even something light, like a balloon, is affected by gravity. Demonstrate by hitting it up in the air and letting it hit the floor.

2. Now explain the game. The object is to beat gravity as long as we can by keeping the balloon in the air. We can count every time it is hit, or time how long we keep it up in the air.

3. To play, give each child or each group of children a balloon. After the game, talk abut the things that children can do to beat gravity. How can they keep the balloon in the air? Can they find ways to improve their time?

Want to do more?

Keep a record and compare performances. Try to discover ways to beat gravity. Study about outer space conditions where no gravity occurs. Use a parachute or sheet to toss and catch the balloon. This is bigger than our hands and becomes a tool to help us do a better job of beating gravity.

FILL 'ER UP

Most children are familiar with gas stations. Some are even familiar with running out of gas. What happens then? The car stops. In this activity, the tricycle stops. FILL 'ER UP uses wheeled toys and water, two all-time favorites, to explore volume, distance, and time. An element of dramatic play holds it all together and allows everyone from oldest to youngest to participate at a meaningful level.

Language with science

out of gas
home safe
full
empty
far
farther
farthest
more
less
fast
slow

Things you will need

paper signs with "out of gas" and "home safe"

water

2 liter bottles with holes punched in the bottom

tricycles

rope or heavy string

What to do

1. Show the children the "gas tanks." Put in some water so they can see how it trickles out.

2. Help tie the bottles on the fronts of the trikes, one per vehicle. This will make it easier for the child to keep an eye on the "gas tank." If they won't fit on the front, tie them on the back. They can still check as they ride.

3. Show them how to fill up the trike with "gas" (water).

4. Off they go! When the "gas" is gone, the trike has to be pushed back. That is the rule. If you can judge when your water is going to be gone and can reach home before you reach empty, then you won't have to push. Before long, the children will be able to judge the volume accurately enough to get the maximum turn.

5. As children return to the fill up station, ask them to point to the sign that tells that they were "out of gas" or "home safe."

Want to do more?

See "Water Clocks" in HUG A TREE. Use cans of varying shapes and sizes, all with the same sized hole. Find some that have different shapes but the same volume, or similar shapes and different volumes. Which one gives you the longest ride? Order the cans by the speed with which they empty. Can you make two different containers empty in the same amount of time? Vary the amount of water or the size or number of holes. Adjustments can be made by plugging holes with modeling clay. If you have two different containers with the same sized hole in the bottom and you pour an equal amount of water in each one, will they both run out at the same time?

ARE YOU ATTRACTED TO ME?

Language with science

magnet
attract
pull
metal

Things you will need

string
magnet

variety of objects
(metal and non
metal) such as:
   paper clips
   pins
   soda cans
   coins
   cotton
   wood
   paper
   another magnet

Certain kinds of metal attract iron and steel. Metals that can do this are called magnets. Magnets are usually made of iron. The iron is made up of tiny, tiny iron atoms. Each iron atom has a small bit of pulling power.

Want another way to work with magnets? Try this one on for size! The important part of this activity is the constant availability of scientific equipment to test inferences about magnetism.

What to do

1. Tie string to magnet. Hang it somewhere in the classroom, i.e., suspend the magnet from a high table. Let the magnet hang so it's approximately 30 cm (1 ft) from the floor.

2. Hold a variety of objects one at a time near the magnet.

3. Observe the magnet closely. When you hold a metal object near, it should move toward the object.

4. Repeat with a variety of objects to learn what objects are attracted.

Want to do more?

Do the same activity only hang two magnets at the same height, approximately 1" apart. Observe what happens. Are magnets attracted to each other? Try to suspend a magnet in space. How many object can you suspend from the magnet? How long a paper clip chain will it hold?

ROLLING ALONG

Language with science

inclined plane
force
inertia
sphere
heavy
light
roll
friction
ramp

Children need to experiment. They need to know that they can find the answers to many questions all by themselves. That's the only way for them to become independent learners, one of the keys to an interesting and exciting life. They best time to introduce this activity is when the children have started constructing their own inclined planes in the block area, such as ramps for their cars. Comparing how far cars roll is a natural beginning. You can then introduce comparing the distance various spheres roll.

When an inclined plane is constructed and spheres are rolled down it, certain physical laws and actions come into play. If the spheres are allowed to roll down the plane, they, just like the cars, will eventually come to rest because of gravity and friction. Does how much a ball weighs or how big it is have an effect on how far it will roll down a hill? This activity lets the children experiment to find the answers.

What to do

1. Set up the inclined plane. Put a line across the upper end to serve as a starting line. If possible, set it up on carpeting, as this will slow the balls down a little and make it easier to keep track of the results.

2. Show the children how to place the balls on the starting line and let them roll by themselves. They will have to practice a little to learn not to push them.

3. Roll each sphere and note where each one stops. You may want to mark the spots with tape or chalk.

4. Can you make a rule for your set of spheres? Some examples are: The heaviest one rolls the farthest. The little balls roll

longer than the big. Help the children explore the ideas by asking questions. Do all marbles roll about the same distance? Which ball is the most fun to roll? Why?

5. Roll the balls again. Are the result about the same?

6. Encourage them to find other balls to roll. Let the children predict where they think one will land and why.

Want to do more?

Switch to a tile floor and note the difference. Roll a small truck down the ramp. What happens when you load it with rocks? Load it with other things and compare. Can you make a rule? What other things can you roll? What about comparing various cylinders such as an oatmeal box and a pencil. What happens when you change the height of the ramp? Older children can graph the results.

WATER MOVERS

Language with science

move
water
siphon
eyedropper
straw
baster
suck
blow
squeeze
release
pull
up
down
vacuum
air pressure

Things you will need

baster
straw
eyedropper

3 to 4 feet of plastic tubing, wide mouthed containers

Children can explore ways to move water from one place to another, and in the process, discover some things about air pressure. When air is removed from a space leaving nothing in its place, the resulting empty space is called a vacuum. Whenever a vacuum is produced, a difference in air pressure results. It is this difference in air pressure that helps us move water in this activity. Each of these liquid moving tools has a unique use. It is fun for the children to find out what works best for them.

What to do

1. Set up 4 separate stations.

   A. Baster and two wide mouthed containers, one full of water, the second empty.

   B. Straw and two wide mouthed containers, one full of water, one empty. Transfer water by putting finger over the end of the straw, not by sucking.

   C. Eyedropper and two wide mouthed containers, one filled with water, one empty.

   D. Plastic tubing and two wide mouthed containers, one filled with water and the other empty. See "Make a Siphon" in **Hodge Podge**.

2. Ask the children how they think we can move water from one container to the next with these different tools. Do they think one tool can move water faster than others? Which one do will take the most effort or work? Which tool will be the easiest to use?

3. Allow the children plenty of time to experiment with the water movers. Coloring or scenting the water can add to the fun.

4. After the children are familiar with the tools, tell them that all of these tools work by using the air around us. When we change the air pressure in the various tools, we create a partial vacuum that causes the water to move. They can get a little more understanding of this idea if they hold a medicine dropper against their skin and squeeze and

release it. This is a big concept. Just share the information informally. Talk about it more if some children are interested. If not, don't belabor the point.

Want to do more?

Let them observe and record on a chart (with teacher assistance) how long it takes to move the water with the various tools. What other tools can we use to move water? Do they all use air pressure, i.e., spoons, cups? Classify water movers — those that use air pressure and those that don't.

SQUARE BALLOONS

Language with science

liquid
shape
mold
freeze
fill
shape names —
square, triangle

Things you will need

water
balloons

various molds,
i.e., square boxes,
square box lids,
milk cartons

Water is a fascinating substance. It can exist in three different forms, as a liquid, as a gas (water vapor), or as a solid (ice). When water is in its liquid form, we can make it into any shape we want. This activity shows us how we can shape water in any way that we please, then by freezing it can make a permanent shape. Permanent, that is, until the temperature starts warming up.

What to do

1. Fill balloons with water and secure by tying neck of balloon in knot.

2. Have children choose molds for their balloons.

3. Place each balloon in a mold and put them in the freezer.

4. Remove from freezer after frozen. Observe that water has been shaped into the form of a square.

5. Have you ever seen a square balloon? Why are these square? What can we do with them? Do you think we can make them round again?

Want to do more?

Collect a variety of molds with a different shape, i.e., cups, round jar lids, pot pie pans. Repeat activity.

KEEP IT WARM

Language with science

insulation
hot
warm
cool
cooler
up
down
cold
wrapped
tighten
test
contains

Things you will need

4 jars with lids
warm water
newspaper
rubber bands
a wool sock
aluminum foil

small box to place jar in

Warm things cool down fast if they are left in cold air because heat travels from warm objects into the cold air quickly. We can help slow down this cooling process by protecting their warmth from the cool air — much in the same way that a warm coat protects us from the cold air when we go outside on a cold day. Like the coat that keeps us warm, the materials we use in this experiment to keep things warm are a form of protection that we call insulation.

What to do

1. Remove lids from jars. Wrap one with a layer of newspaper. Hold the newspaper in place with rubber bands. Place one jar in a box and place crumpled newspaper loosely around it. Tie a sock around the third jar. Leave the fourth jar unwrapped.

2. Fill each jar with very warm water. Let the children test the warmth of the water by placing their fingers in it. All four jars should be equal in warmth.

3. Place lids back on jars and leave the jars alone for 15 minutes.

4. Take off the jar lids and let children test the water with their little finger.

5. Which jar contains the warmest water?

Want to do more?

Do the same activity with a thermometer. For younger children, have them look at the height of the red line — is it higher or lower than when we started? Try different types of insulation, i.e., paper towel, toilet paper, kleenex, clay, or rags. Encourage the children to experiment with their own ideas. Conduct an insulation hunt in a grocery or hardware store.

STATIC ELECTRICITY TESTER

Language with science

electricity
static electricity
attract

Things you will need

static electricity tester — created by suspending a cork on a string and painting it with metallic paint. Push the string in with a nail, add white glue to the string, and allow to dry.

Static electricity producing objects: wool rug, rabbit fur, small piece of dry cleaner plastic, chamois, plastic spoons, piece of nylon, styrofoam, etc., comb

Static electricity is the result of a condition created on a substance's surface in which electrons are either in excess or deficient. The presence of electron imbalance causes the movement of static electricity or electrons from one object to another when brought into contact. An attempt is made by both objects to be neutral, that is, not to have a deficiency or excess. When we walk across a rug, rubbing our feet, we create that excess/deficiency. The result is a static electricity shock when we touch something, and the electrons move to create balance. Many static electricity conditions exist. Our evidence is the spark (shock), but there is a way to test the presence of static electricity, the invisible force. Try it out!

What to do

1. Suspend the static electricity tester from the ceiling in a place where it is out of the way.

2. Show how the static electricity machine works. Take the comb and comb hair. Place the comb close to the tester. The static electricity passes to the tester causing it to turn. It's an invisible passing of energy from one object to another.

3. Place the objects that form static electricity in a learning center and allow the students to create static electricity. Then test it.

Want to do more?

Bring in static retardant to spray static electricity creating materials. Does it work? Experiment with anything the children can think of that will cause static electricity to be created.

WATER DROP RACE

Language with science

water
water dropper
race
wax paper
fast
faster
fastest
watch
observe

Things you will need

cookie sheet

small containers of colored water

empty container

wax paper to cover ramp

eyedroppers

Water is a wonderful liquid. Not only does it form the major material present on this earth, but it is the primary component of all living things. Then to top that off, it is the best solvent and the best solution we know of in chemistry. It is free for us to use, to misuse, and to treasure. What makes water so wonderful are its properties of cohesion and adhesion. We can see this when we drop water on wax paper. Cohesion is the ability of substances to stick to themselves. Just drop water on the wax paper. Add another drop and another drop. The drops stay together until gravity pulls them down, but they do stay together. Adhesion is the ability to stick to a different substance. Just add water to a waxed surface and see how it sticks. Add more drops and more drops, finally the drop will be heavy enough to glide to the ground. But some of it usually is strongly adhesive enough to stick to the surface.

What to do

1. Attach wax paper to the cookie sheet.

2. Tip cookie sheet at a slight angle. Rest one end on a block or book.

3. The children each need to mix a favorite color of water and food coloring.

4. Put a line of drops of water on the wax paper. The children continue to add to the original droplets until the water begins to run down the board. How many drops does it take before it runs? Does one color run faster than the other?

Want to do more?

Add soap to the water. Repeat the process and compare the number of drops it takes before the water begins to run down. Do the drops run faster or slower? Experiment with the angle of the plane. Try the same activity on a plane without wax paper. Try this same experiment with different liquids: vinegar, liquid soap, milk.

PULLEY THINGS ALONG

Language with science

pulley
lift
machine
work

Things you will need

2 spools
2 coat hangers

long piece of string

small basket

A pulley is a special type of wheel which has a rim for a rope to fit into. Its purpose is to help us lift and move things that are heavy from one place to another. It is a simple machine that is easy for young children to construct and find application for in the school yard. The pulley is a machine; it is designed to do work. If your reason for building this machine is to transport some important objects such as blocks across the wide abyss of your classroom to the heights of the climber, then the pulley machine your class builds will do a wonderful job. For the children to see the advantage of constructing and using the machine they build, it must make work easier. In other words, there must be some advantage in using the pulley machine.

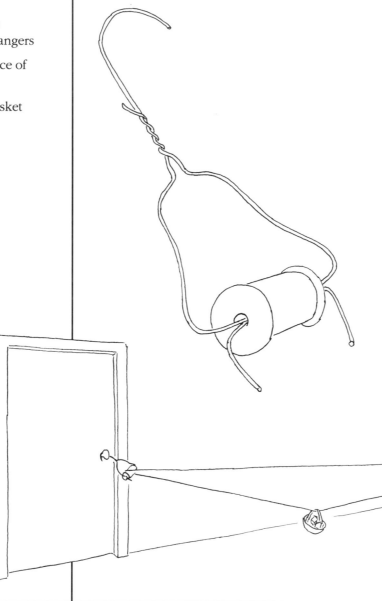

What to do

1. With the children, construct the pulley system, using the drawing as your design.

2. Set up the pulley system in the classroom.

3. Select objects to place in the pulley system and transport across the classroom.

4. Which objects will cause the pulley system to break down or not work? What could you do to make a better system or one that would carry more weight?

Want to do more?

Develop a pulley system that would pull a load straight up, instead of across. Can you pull a greater load that way? Buy some small pulleys at the hardware store and compare them to the ones you have made.

PENDULUM BOWL

Language with science

pendulum
swing
angle

Things you will need

a string

a heavy square or round object to serve as the bob

7-10 small empty plastic containers such as film cannisters or pill bottles

A pendulum's swing is controlled by the laws of physics. That swing is in a straight line and its return is dependent on the angle from which it has been released. Knowing a bit of science is a real benefit for the players in this game. A teacher who wishes to encourage the problem solving ability of children will allow plenty of time for experimentation, then explain that rules of geometry and physics determine the exact path and return of the pendulum. Show the children that rule and allow them to see the rule in practice. They can experience a practical reason to know a little science.

What to do

1. Tie up the pendulum so it just clears the ground under a swing, tree, or table. Make the pendulum string length about 1.5 meters.

2. Place the empty plastic containers in bowling order. See drawing.

3. Introduce the rules for the game.

   A. 3 turns at releasing the pendulum.

   B. Total the number of containers knocked over.

   C. Keep score, resetting containers after 3 turns.

4. As you play, talk about the route of the pendulum and its return. The pendulum can knock down containers on the way over and on its return.

Want to do more?

See "Reflection Connection" in this chapter and "Satellite Signal Sender" in the **Flight and Space** chapter. Send the pendulum over so it hits the containers on the return swing only. Experiment with the length of the string.

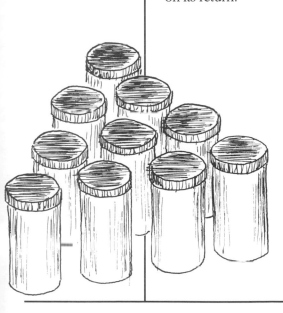

BUILD YOUR
OWN ROLLER COASTER

A popular toy for children of all ages is the marble runner game. These little items can cost a small fortune. Instead, let children build their own marble runner by using cardboard tubes and other throw-aways. This tube building activity is an application of all the ramp and inclined plane teaching you have been doing. Knowledge of motion and reaction of mass to gravity are applied as the children see the ball shoot out because the angle is too great on one tube and not enough on another. Trial and error will begin this very practical activity, but that will lead to more experimenting and testing of this simple apparatus.

Language with science

ramp
roll
angle
plan
experiment
tube
cylinder

Things you will need

cardboard tubes from wrapping paper, toilet paper, etc.

lightweight cardboard (old file folders)

plastic wrap
aluminum foil
tape
marbles

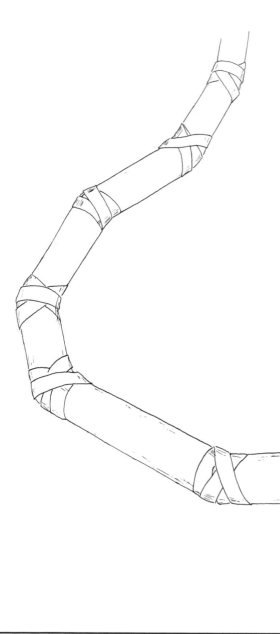

What to do

1. Have a child climb up to highest spot safely reachable in the classroom such as the top of a climber. Tape a wrapping paper tube at an angle to the wall, climber, or whatever. Below the opening of the first tube, tape a second tube, and so forth down to the ground.

2. As a marble is placed in the top it will roll down the first tube. If the first and second tubes are placed at proper locations and angles, the marble will continue to roll down. Too much angle and it will shoot out; too little and it stops. Problem solving becomes the key to this activity.

Want to do more?

Add devices such as gates where bells are rung or noises made; long runs can be slowed by uphill changes, or directions can be changed by having the marble hit something solid and bounce off into another channel. What is the longest track you can make?

THE HOLE IN THE STRAW TRICK

Language with science

air pressure
suction

Things you will need

straws
pin or knife

glasses full of water or juice for each child

Straws and atomizers all work because of air pressure. The air presses down on us like a giant blanket all over the earth. It presses on us, and it presses on liquid in a glass. When the children suck, it causes uneven pressure and the air pushes the water higher into the straw. Put a hole in the straw and the pressure is equal everywhere.

What to do

1. With a sharp object, place a hole in each of the straws at various levels from the bottom. Start at one centimeter from the bottom and move up the straw by one centimeter intervals. Have several at each level and leave one or two with no holes.

2. Place one straw in each glass of water or juice. Naturally, the children will drink.

3. Soon the children will discover that there is a problem. The children will suck harder or will ask why the straw is not working. Some children will empty their glasses. Why?

4. We can now discover what the difference is. The hole created the problem. When the hole was under liquid, the straw worked. If we cover up the hole, will it work again? Try that solution! Yes, it works. Okay, teacher, no more pranks! But at least you know why your straw doesn't work and how to fix it.

Want to do more?

See "Water Movers" in this chapter. Try "Make a Siphon" in **Hodge Podge**.

THE REFLECTION DIRECTION

Language with science

reflect
ray of light
communication
bounce off

Things you will need

flat even mirror
flashlight
tennis ball

Remember in the cartoons and movies how signals from distant hills or rooftops were flashed to send messages to friendly forces? Reflections of mirrors or other bright objects have historically been one way for people to communicate over great distances. Earth and space communications are based on this same principle. Just as a light can be reflected by a mirror to be seen at a distant spot, space stations will reflect their light and communication signals to earth stations. Learning how mirrors reflect light is the beginning of an understanding of how many communication devices work.

What to do

1. Explain that when a tennis ball is thrown against a wall at an angle, it bounces off at about the same angle. Let the children try it.

2. Explain that when a light is projected against a mirror at an angle, it bounces off at about the same angle, just as the ball did.

3. Let the children try it using the flashlight and the mirror.

4. Let the children move to different spots in the room as they repeat the process. Observe the new direction that the reflected rays take.

5. Turn the mirror slightly and notice how the angles change.

6. Allow them to experiment and learn to predict where the beam of light will hit.

Want to do more?

What surfaces other than mirrors could be used to reflect light? For example, water, windows, utensils, bottles, cans, foil. See "Flashlight Tag" in MUDPIES TO MAGNETS.

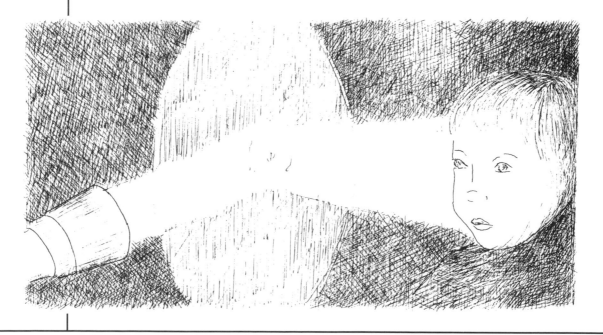

DIGGING IN THE DIRT:
EARTH EXPLORATIONS

DIGGING IN THE DIRT: EARTH EXPLORATIONS

Geology is
- the study of the properties of matter composing the planetary bodies, the way that matter is formed and interacts, including the nature and development of land form, both historically, and as we know it today.
- people studying the way the earth and other planetary bodies are formed. Because all planetary bodies are made up of great quantities of rocks, geologists spend much time in the studies of rocks and soils.

Ideas to share with children
- Through geology we have found huge gas and coal deposits that fuel your cars and warm your houses. The iron, steel, copper, aluminum, and other metals in cars, buildings, and coins were mined from rocks that geologists found.
- Geologists tell people where it is safe to build roads, houses, and dams. They know how the earth moves and changes over time. Earthquakes that shake our cities can cause huge damage, and geologists are trying to determine when and how they occur.
- A geologist who studies soil can help farmers, homeowners, and park developers by analyzing the soil and telling what plants will best grow there. We lose much soil by erosion each year, and geology can help tell us how to prevent this.

Things to do
- Bring in collections of rocks, minerals, gems, soils, sands, and fossils to have the children observe the variety in these samples. A parent may have some background in geology and would share that knowledge with the class.
- Geology laboratories are not always easy to find, but geology applications can be seen in rock shops, concrete and gravel operations, brick yards, and quarries. Colleges usually have geology labs and collections. Buildings in your city will have been constructed with a wide variety of stone materials. Observing these during field trips is interesting.
- If you want to focus on geology and earth science, and you want to dress the part; find a rock hammer, collecting bag, safety glasses, and a few rocks. Geologists, however, usually turn to chemistry and physics to really study rocks.
- Local field trips to compare and study soils and rocks are available. Try walks through a road cut, along a stream bed or lakeshore, in new building construction where a foundation has been dug, or along driveways or rock displays at landscape companies.

- Soil conservation services exist in each area of your state or province. Their job is to help save soil. Soil conservationists will provide you with information, samples and presentations.
- Famous geologists are A. Wegener, Louis Agassiz, and William Smith.
- The following geology ideas can be found in:

HUG A TREE

A Piece of Our World
Nuts for You and Rocks, Too
Bury the Sock
Old and New
Wash Out

MUDPIES TO MAGNETS

Minimuseum
Put a Rock to Bed
Cave in a Box
Turning Mudpies into Houses
Puddle Walk
Sensitive Toes
Ocean in a Jar

WATER FLOW

Language with science

force
flow
float
movement

Things you will need

water hose

objects of various size, shape, or weight (have some the size of a brick)

sidewalk or long table

Children enjoy the fun and excitement of playing with a hose while helping mom or dad wash the car or water the garden. This activity builds on that experience as it demonstrates how the force of water can move objects, both small and large.

What to do

1. Place the objects you have collected on the sidewalk.

2. Turn on the hose and tell the children to move the objects to the end of the sidewalk. They should be given time to play as you help them focus on what happens to each of the objects as they spray the water.

3. Let each child have a turn at moving the objects with the water. Why are some things easier to move than others?

4. Go on a field trip to a stream bed or area where water flows. Compare what objects move with the ones that lay still in the stream or waterflow area.

5. Make a list of objects in the stream bed or flow area which move easily and which may not move easily.

6. Take some objects back to class to try in your own "stream."

Want to do more?

Change the velocity of water by adding a nozzle. Find a culvert or ditch or drain. Use the hose in the enclosed space, or place bricks together to make a ditch or trough. Make a dam in the ditch. See what large amounts of water do to move objects. Do some things make better dams than others?

SAND SHAKE

Language with science

tide
flow
settle
silt
dunes

Things you will need

small clear jars — clear, plastic spice jars work well

sand of different textures that is free of dirt or silt

water

A walk along a creek bed, a river bank, or the ocean beach reveals that sand and soil are deposited in various layers at the water's edge. As water moves down a river, it carries huge amounts of silt and sand. When the water slows, the sand is deposited in layers. As the tides flow, rising and falling, they carry deposits of sand along the beach. As the sand is deposited it is shaped as the water slows and settles. While this experiment does not show that rippled form, it does shows that sand settles in many different ways. Leave the jars out for the children to use. They have a fascinating quality and can be just the thing to settle active children.

What to do

1. Fill the jars with half sand and half water. Leave 2 cm (1/2 inch) of air space on the top.

2. Give the jars to the children to shake.

3. Watch the sand as it settles.

4. Compare the various jars of sand to see if they are the same or different. What happens?

Want to do more?

Compare sand collected in different locations. Try various kinds of jars. Which do you like the best. Pour dirt into a jar with water and watch as it is shaken and allowed to settle. Add objects to the sand to change the pattern. Imagine it is a shell washing on the beach. Does it change how the sand settles?

DON'T BE ROUGH, BE SMOOTH: MAKE SANDPAPER

Language with science

sand
sandpaper
large
small
smaller
fine
grit
rough
smooth

Discuss carpentry tools that carpenters use. Where does sand come from? Is it dirty or clean? How can you tell? Can we wash it? How?

Things you will need

file folders
white glue
sand of varying sizes
pieces of wood
real sandpaper

One of our jobs as teachers of science is to make children aware of how scientists have taken ordinary things and created useful materials. The children can, in this case, make and use the product to do work. So let us roll up our sleeves and get the assembly line going because we have work to do.

What to do

1. Show the children the various grades of sandpaper. Give them plenty of time with the wood and sandpaper to see how the various grades work.

2. How do you think we could make our own sandpaper? Accept their ideas and try them out. Supply the glue, sand, and pieces of file folder and let them experiment.

3. When their sandpaper is complete and the glue is dry, let them try out their experiments. Most of them will not work particularly well. Do they have any ideas for improvement? Give them a try. You might explain to them that at sandpaper factories there are special machines that spread the glue and the sand very evenly. That's why we usually buy sandpaper. It works better.

4. When sandpaper production is complete, suggest making a group wood sculpture. Let each child choose a piece of wood to sand as desired, with the sandpaper of their choice — homemade or commercial. Make a base of several large pieces of wood glued together. Then let the children add their own pieces, as they wish. Some children get upset about a piece being glued on top of theirs. You can talk about all the pieces working together to make one scupture to help ease the strain.

Want to do more?

Encourage the children to make individual sculptures. Bring in a variety of sandpapers and woods. A note home will bring lots of contributions. Bring in paste wax so they can polish the wood when it's sanded smooth.

SORTING ROCKS IN THE SOIL

Language with science

matching
rock
light
medium
dark
long
thin
flat
colors
rough
smooth

Things you will need

rock collection with pairs of similar rocks

shoe boxes

Sorting and classifying can be lots of fun when the children are involved in both hiding and finding the materials. This activity enables them to develop vocabulary, matching, and memory skills as they play a different form of concentration that is both fun as well as informative. The children can hide and find all of the rocks you put in your sand pile. Make sure the pairs are distinct at first. As the children become more skilled, you can throw in some tough matches.

What to do

1. Go to the sand box and hide the rock pairs before the children arrive.

2. Prepare the children by saying that the rocks that we have studied during the past week were buried by a tremendous land slide in the sand box. There are two of each kind of rock.

3. This is sand box concentration. Find a rock, find another one like it, and you have made a match. Take the two out.

4. Check with your teacher or a friend to see if the match is correct.

5. Continue until all matches are made.

Want to do more?

With older children, play concentration. They have to rebury each rock in its place until they find the match.

FLOATING ICEBERGS

Language with science

float
iceberg
ice
freeze
water

Things you will need

food coloring

various shaped bowls and containers

wading or swimming pool

large freezer

A regular phenomena of the arctic world of our continent is the production of icebergs. Some of the children may have knowledge of the Titanic's sinking by an iceberg through the song. While the iceberg may not be a part of everyone's experiences, a hot day and a dip in the pool do provide an opportunity to experiment firsthand with treading safely through vast sea lanes strewn with huge chunks of ice that upon contact will crush the hull of your fragile boat. Or cool you off.

What to do

1. Fill the containers with water. Add food coloring. Place in the freezer and allow to freeze completely.

2. Take the frozen containers out, remove the ice, and place the icebergs in the pool. Notice how much of the ice is under water.

3. Have the children place their hands near the iceberg and move them away. How far does the cold water extend from the ice?

4. Watch the shape of the iceberg as it melts. Does the shape change?

Want to do more?

See "Square Balloons" in the **First Physics** chapter and "Ice Cube Necklaces" in the **Weather Watchers** chapter. How long does the iceberg take to melt? Does the color and size make a difference? Freeze objects inside your iceberg and see how long it takes for them to melt free. Do other liquids float when frozen? Try indoors in water table with toy boats.

PIE PAN CRYSTAL BUILDING

Language with science

crystal
solution
dissolve
stir
mixture
rocks
stones
salt
evaporate

Things you will need

glass or ceramic
pie plate (salt will
corrode metal)

rocks of various
sizes

water
salt
collecting bags

A crystal is a three dimensional structure that repeats itself. We see crystals in snowflakes, quartz rocks, and rock candy. Heat, pressure, and time change (or metamorphize) rock to create the less abundant, although more beautiful, crystals such as opal, ruby, garnet and diamond. We cannot make these in our laboratories, but we can make other crystals. This activity shows the children how to build a pie pan crystal structure using salt that is mixed with water and allowed to dry. Crystal upon crystal is formed as the water slowly evaporates over a period of several days.

What to do

1. Take a rock collecting walk. Collect rocks of various sizes, enough to 3/4 fill a pie pan.

2. Mix 2 tablespoons of salt with 1/4 cup of warm tap water.

3. After the salt dissolves completely, pour the mixture over the rocks in the pan.

4. Place the pan on a window sill so it receives direct sunlight.

5. Let the children observe and talk about what they see as the crystals form.

Want to do more?

Try using larger amounts of salt, use food coloring to make different colors. What else can you use to grow crystals? Try all suggestions. Which ones work and which don't?

STIR–IN FOSSILS

Fossils are imprints of plants and animals that died long ago and were preserved in the earth. This activity provides a hands-on method of discovering a little about how real fossils are made.

What to do

1. Fill a container half full of soil. Mix water with soil, stirring until you have a thick consistency — mud that can be molded or shaped by hand. Stir the object or objects into the mixture.

NOTE: This activity works best with soil that has a high clay content. Very rich soil, like potting soil, will crumble too easily. Try it with the soil you have chosen before using it with the children.

2. Pour out onto wax paper placed on a cookie sheet. Now form a mudpie, making sure that the stirred-in objects are totally concealed in the mud.

3. Place the mudpies on a window sill or outside so the sun can aid in the drying process. Let sit for a full day and overnight. Check after 24 hours to see if it is dried throughout. If you've been unfortunate enough to do this activity in very humid weather, you might want to put the mudpies in an oven on low heat to finish drying.

4. When thoroughly dry, let children take a mudpie and carefully break it open, preferably with their hands.

5. Observe and discuss the imprints (fossils) that they have made. Remember these fossils were made in a day or two, while real fossils took millions of years to form.

Want to do more?

Take a walk along a dry creek bed. See if you can find some real fossils or bring in fossils to show. Do rubbings of fossils. Discuss dinosaurs and fossils the children have brought from home to share — an excellent activity to introduce the concept of time passing. Discuss places where we can find fossils.

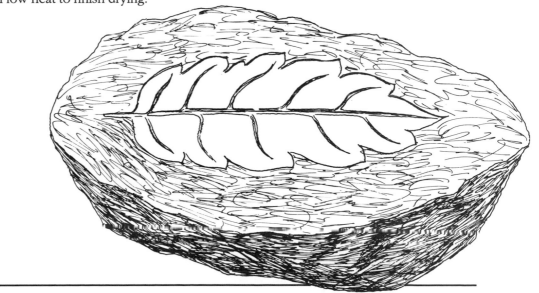

PET ROCKS ON PARADE

Language with science

mineral
rock
properties
texture
appearance
shiny
layered
old
color

Things you will need

rocks from the children

rock sets

dried grass

leaves

sticks

egg cartons (cut into thirds)

magnifiers

Rock collecting is one phase of exploring the environment that all children seem to find interesting. A shiny rock from a stream, a piece of glistening stone from the hundreds on a mountain side or seashore find their way back from vacations to be stuck on shelves or placed in boxes and forgotten over time. Too bad. So let us give children a reason to return those rocks to use. We can use their rocks, and their interest to observe, classify, and describe those forgotten treasures of times gone by.

What to do

1. Ask the children to bring in rocks to show their friends.

2. Provide various materials, natural or manmade, so each child can create a home for his or her rock. A natural "Rock Bed" might be dried grass, a nice leaf or two, and sticks to make the rock feel at home.

3. Each child is then encouraged to tell the rock's story. The story can be real or pretend.

4. Place the rocks on display in the science center for continued sharing. Some children might enjoy using magnifiers for a closer look.

Want to do more?

Rocks can be grouped and classified. Compare them to rock collections. Visit a geology display or a lapidary shop. What is your state rock or mineral? How do the rocks change when they are wet?

THE ACID TEST

One way we classify rocks is by their appearance. Another way is to observe their reaction to chemicals. One group of rocks (limestone) has a particular chemical make-up that allows it to react with an acid to give off carbon dioxide, a gas. This group is sedimentary in origin and was formed as a result of deposits of dead organic materials on the ocean floors. Most limestone was formed by marine animals with calcium bodies (a bone-like material). Although changed over time by temperature and pressure, the limestone materials all react to acid by releasing carbon dioxide (CO_2). Bubbles are given off. If the acid is strong enough, the rock fizzes when it is touched. So now you have a way to identify limestone.

Language with science

geologist
rocks
collection
collect
quartz
limestone
clay
kaolinite
calcite
marble
chalk
vinegar
compare
test
reaction
acid test

Things you will need

plastic cups
white vinegar
paint chip samples

collection of rocks, i.e., quartz, limestone, kaolinite (a common constituent of clay), calcite, white marble, chalk

What to do

1. Have children bring an assortment of rocks from home. Also have an assortment on hand that you have collected.

2. Compare the rocks by observing their similarities. Tell the children that geologists compare rocks by looking at them and also by testing them. One way of testing is to compare rocks by color — do this using paint chip samples.

3. Another way that geologists test rocks is to see if they contain calcium carbonate. We can be geologists today. Put a different rock in each cup. Pour warm white vinegar to cover the rock.

4. Watch closely to see which rocks form bubbles and fizz. Some of the rocks fizz more than others. Why?

5. Name the rocks that react to the vinegar and those that don't.

Want to do more?

Cover the rocks with vinegar for 24 hours. Are any of the rocks affected by the vinegar? How? Discuss the geologist profession, the many differences and similarities of rocks, some of which are observable, some that are not, unless some form of testing is induced.

HIGH TIDE WIPE OUT

Language with science

tide
high tide
low tide
shore
beach

Things you will need

sticks
tide
tide schedules

Everyone who has been to the ocean and seen the tide ebb and flow knows the power that is expended each day by its effort. We know from our beach experiences that tides vary in their intensity and height. But how much and on what tide? Let's find out!

What to do

1. Walk along the beach at high tide collecting sticks to use as markers.

2. Select a quiet spot for your experiment that does not get much traffic.

3. Find where the high tide line is. You can tell this mark because it will be the high point on the beach where many algae, dry grass, seaweed, and other flotsam are pushed up by the highest tides and storms.

4. Begin at high tide and push a stick into the sand. Push them in 2-4 inches (10 cm) in a straight line toward the ocean every foot (30 cm) apart. Put 10-15 sticks in the sand.

5. Return the day after the high tide and check the point where the tide has washed the sticks out. Where the sticks stand the tide did not reach in strength.

6. Readjust sticks and begin the next day's observation.

Want to do more?

Place sticks deep in the sand to see the strength of the tide at varying depths. Place objects of varying size and shape to see what the tide does to them and their location.

INSTANT VOLCANO

One of those experiments that every child should do is to make a play volcano. TV cartoons are full of pictures of cities, societies, and jungle camps being overrun by lava, so most children have some visual images of volcanic lava flow. We can't duplicate the hot, molten activity of a true lava flow. We can pretend that it is happening, and, of course, we can replicate this volcanic activity on demand.

Language with science

volcano
chemical reaction
carbon dioxide
gas
vinegar
baking soda
erupt
combine
mix
build
play
make believe
dormant
quiet
lava

Things you will need

soup cans
vinegar
water
baking soda
teaspoon
food coloring
(red)

sand,

soil or leaves

clay (to be used
to build a mound
around the vol-
cano)

What to do

1. Place the can on the ground outside or on a paper plate or tray, if inside.

2. Have children build a mound around the can using soil, sand, leaves, clay, or paper to create their own image of a small mountain.

3. Fill the can 1/2 to 3/4 full with vinegar. Add a few drops of red food coloring, then a spoonful of baking soda.

4. Watch the lava flow down the sides of the volcano as the chemical reaction between the acid and the baking soda occurs.

5. Repeat as long as the vinegar, baking soda, and interest lasts.

Want to do more?

What other acids can we mix with baking soda to create carbon dioxide? Try fruit juice (lemon concentrate), milk, water. Which one do you think contains acid?

I'M FINE

Language with science

fine
very fine
ultrafine
very coarse
coarse
chunky

Things you will need

pieces of chalk

plastic glasses or goggles

hammer

The size of rocks, minerals, ores, pearls, and gems are all graded by particle size. Ordering by size allows engineers to develop machinery to sort materials as they are used. While the technology may not be within the scope of most of our children, the idea that people use size to sort out materials is well within their grasp. Besides that, children love to pound things, so this should be a fine lesson.

What to do

1. Have the child or several children take several pieces of chalk out to the sidewalk and break them up into chunks, then break some of the chunks up, and so on until some of the chalk has been reduced to dust. Be sure the children wear glasses to protect their eyes.

2. With the children, order the chalk pieces by size from fine to the coarsest size. Discuss the words listed as the ordering takes place. Attach these words to the sizes and discuss how scientists might use these words to differentiate and describe different sizes of gravel, ore, or sand for sandpaper. Can they think of different ways to use the various grades of chalk?

Want to do more?

Find gravel and with various sizes of wire screen determine the fineness of the gravel. Bring in a variety of sandpaper and let the children grade them. Try the samples on wood. What is the difference? Sift sand from the sandbox.

HEAD NORTH, CHILD, NORTH

Language with science

north
south
east
west
compass
direction
line

Things you will need

compass

signs for north, south, east, and west

chalk

To the young child, compasses are toys. They are included in "little camper" and "little explorer" play sets as props for make-believe play. The quality may not be great, but most of them do work with at least some degree of accuracy. The trouble is that not many adults and even fewer children know how to use them. This activity will not teach the children to find their way in the woods, but it will show them in yet another way that some things in our world are consistent and predictable. The needle on a compass always points north.

What to do

1. Explain to the children that certain words give directions — some we use commonly such as up, down, toward, beside.

2. Four words that show direction to scientists who study weather and the earth are north, south, east, and west. North is the direction we are going to explore.

3. Lay the compass on the floor so the needle is lined up on north. It would be good to have the compass located so it points to an open door or window on a north wall.

4. With chalk, draw a line extending north from the compass.

5. Ask several of the children to walk north on the line.

6. Go to the end of the line; lay the compass down again. Extend the north line out as far as you can go, each time laying the compass down to check the direction.

7. The direction north goes on and on. It is a direction one finds when a compass is used to point the way.

8. Do the same activity the next day. With several repetitions, the children will discover that a compass always works in the same way. Walking on all those lines won't hurt either. You could even let them pick the direction of the day. What do you need to do to make a zigzag walking line?

Want to do more?

Add the directions east, south, and west. Label the walls of the classroom in the appropriate direction. Look at maps of the area. Find the direction symbols. Locate directions on a walk you take. A compass works everywhere you go.

MUDDY MUDDY RIVER

Language with science

streams
rivers
beaches
moving water
erode
change
sediment
silt

Things you will need

clear containers
(all the same size)

lids if you intend
to save the water

a can suspended
from the end of a
pole

One of the great changers of the earth's surface is water. Its flow over soil and rock slowly and continuously erodes and remakes the land. Even what appears to be clear water contains sediment which is carried along as the water moves. Tremendous amounts of soil are moved in spring and wet season runoffs. Some rivers are named for the colors created by the soils carried in their flowing waters. By watching sediment settle out of the water you collect, children will see that even water that looks clean has dirt in it. That's one reason we drink only purified water.

What to do

1. Find a stream or river edge where moving water can be collected. Try to choose one where the water is particularly muddy. Clear streams will have heavier silt loads during high water.

CAUTION: The safety factor in drawing the water is paramount. A long stick with a can on the end allows you to reach into the water and maintain a safe distance from the water's edge. You should choose your water selection site carefully. It may be best to have only adults collect the water.

2. Pour the collected water into a clear container. Label it with the water source.

3. Allow the water to settle. Observe the sediment as it settles out. Even the clearest moving water will have small amounts of tiny soil particles. If the water is very clear, use a white plastic cup to hold the water.

Want to do more?

Repeat with several water sources. Have the children bring a water sample from a family outing. Enclose a label so the family can fill in the water source and any other interesting information. Repeat in the same location, but during different flow rates, such as before and after a rain. Allow water you have collected to evaporate. Compare the results with evaporated tap water.

CLEANING MUDDY WATER

Language with science

filter
clean
remove
clear
pure

Things you will need

500 ml (1 pint) jar full of muddy water with sticks floating in it

sand

rocks

tops of 2 liter soda bottles (see drawing)

a large, clear container

It's an awesome problem to be thirsty and be faced with dirty water. First imagine how it would be. Have you ever been that thirsty? Your lips would be chapped and cracked. It would be terrible to be that thirsty and faced with this glass of water (hold up a muddy container of water). What would you do? Would you drink the water? I wouldn't; I would clean it by using a natural filter made from things I can find outside. Would you like to try making a water filter to remove the mud from the water? Of course, the water you have cleaned won't be completely clean. It will still contain microscopic creatures, such as bacteria and other one celled organisms. To really complete the cleansing, drop in iodine tablets specially made to purify water. In 30 minutes the water will be ready to drink, crystal clear. Or you can boil the water, at a fast boil for 15 minutes, cool, and drink.

What to do

1. Use the discussion in the introduction to develop interest in clean water.

2. Elicit suggestions for cleaning the dirty water in the jar.

3. Suggest you might have a way that will work and offer this demonstration:

A. Place the top of the soda container upside down in a glass.

B. Add a layer of crushed rock. Arrange one rock so it plugs up the open end (2 cm deep).

C. Pour in sand (2 cm).

D. Place "funnel" into a large, clear container to collect the cleaned water.

4. Add, with gusto, the dirty water. Shake the jar well to make sure that nothing is settled on the bottom.

5. Watch as the clear water comes out of the "funnel." What happened to all the dirt? Can you find it?

Want to do more?

Evaporate to see if there is still stuff left in the water.

DIGGING IN THE DIRT

Language with science

dig
dirt
soil
paleontologist
sample
measure

Things you will need

shovels
trowels
meter stick
baby food jars

Most children love to play in the dirt. This activity takes advantage of this natural vehicle of play and lets it unfold into a geological experience that involves digging, collecting, labeling, and recording data in a scientific way. Paleontologists use this process when they unearth dinosaur bones. Many children's books about dinosaurs illustrate such a dig. While you probably won't find dinosaur bones, you'll never know what's there waiting for you until you start to dig.

What to do

1. Select a spot in the school yard or in an adjacent vacant lot. Have the children bring the digging tools.

2. With the meter stick, measure and mark a square meter. Begin to dig your hole within the square.

3. At each 10 or 15 cm (4 to 6 in) level, collect a baby food jar full of soil. Label the jars with the depth. Save anything else you find — rocks, snail shells, roots, worms.

4. Dig as deep as you wish. Can you identify the things you've found? Compare the various soil samples. Make a miniature museum with your finds. Label them with all the information you have. Keep living things for only 24 hours, then return them to the hole.

5. Return the dirt to the hole. Does it fit? Pack the dirt down by stepping on it. Discuss how compaction changes soil and how digging loosens it.

6. Have each of the children bring a soil sample from home. They are to note the collection depth and location.

7. Bring the samples and compare with the school yard samples. Do any match?

Want to do more?

Call the local soil conservation department to bring out soil samples. Make a soil collection. Make a sand collection. Find a road cut where a soil profile can be seen. Bring in fossils to share with the children. Visit the geology department at a nearby museum or college.

5+ COAL: A VERY SPECIAL ROCK

Language with science

rock
coal
hardness
streak
luster (shiny)
fuel
geologist

Things you will need

chunks of coal
white construction paper

a hammer

newsprint
rocks

One of our most important sources of energy is coal. It is the fossil remains of plants buried millions of years ago. Under pressure and heat of the soil deposited over them, the plants compressed, hardened, and changed colors to form coal. Like oil, coal is a fossil fuel. Most children know nothing about it. While coal is harder to find than ordinary gravel rocks, most areas have a place where it is available. Check the yellow pages and pick up enough for each child to have a piece to study. This activity provides the children with hands-on interaction with this very special kind of rock.

What to do:

1. Place a piece of coal in each child's hand.

2. Tell them this is a rock that they are about to study and it is a very special one because it gives us heat and light. It is coal. Discuss how coal was once used to heat almost every home and is still used in some homes for heat. It also is burned in power plants, and its energy converted to electricity. This activity uses coal to introduce how rocks are studied by geologists.

3. Look at the chart below and ask the children for their observations. Record these on a newsprint sheet. Older children can keep individual data sheets.

4. Let each child find another rock and go through the same process. This is the kind of procedure a geologist follows to identify a new specimen.

Want to do more?

Use a match or lighter to light a small piece of coal. Study other rocks: limestone, sandstone, granite. Compare to charcoal.

	SMELL	FEEL	LOOK	COLOR	HIT WITH HAMMER	MARK ON PAPER
COAL						
MY ROCK						

HOW HOT, HOW COLD, HOW WINDY, HOW WET: WEATHER WATCHERS

HOW HOT, HOW COLD, HOW WINDY, HOW WET: WEATHER WATCHERS

Meteorology is

- the study of the atmosphere, particularly as it is related to the study and prediction of weather.
- studied by persons called meteorologists and climatologists. They work to understand the functions of weather and climate and their affect on each other.

Ideas to share with children

- Meteorologists may be the people who give us weather information on the television news. Their job is to analyze weather patterns and predict what new weather will be. The job of the meteorologist is enhanced by the use of computers and weather satellites. Because they know what weather has done in the past, these scientists hope they can predict what it will do in the future. That prediction is very difficult because we do not always have good or sufficient data from the past.
- Some meteorologists are studying how weather is affected in a very small place, such as a city or valley. Others are studying how weather is happening all over the world. Our look at the greenhouse effect and the ozone layer are examples of global studies. Some scientists are even studying weather patterns on other planets and comparing them to earth.
- Weather is a concern for all of us because it affects our work, play, and feelings. Some weather subjects are clouds, rain, snow, hurricanes, tornadoes, temperatures, and sun. If we know about the weather, we know how to dress and how to live. Weather is very important to our everyday lives.

Things to do

- Most children will be involved with a weather unit some time in their schooling. While the unit on weather is very applicable to everyday lives, it is a very abstract for children. Weather happens, but it has some predictability. In order to study the events of weather, data must be collected, so charts on weather events are a must.
- Weather safety lessons may save a child's life. Hurricane and tornado drills should be associated with some weather information. Choosing the proper clothing for given weather situations might be coupled with general information on "what to do in case of." Talk about hypothermia, sudden storms, sunburn, and other weather related problems, but not all at once! Follow seasonal changes and the related problems.
- Many television newsroom personalities will come to schools to talk about their jobs and about weather. Not too many weather field trips can be taken, but one could be to the television station or to the weather room at the airport. Pilots are very concerned about weather and may be willing to share information. You can take a weather walk and discover how weather affects plants, animals, and the soil.

- If you want to focus on meteorology, then surround yourself with the tools and data of the trade. Contact the National Weather Service for maps, charts, and tables. Collect thermometers, anemometers, wind vanes, barometers, and hygrometers. Add cloud pictures and bunches of weather maps from local and national papers to your array and try to predict tomorrow's weather. Don't forget to tune in to the local weather radio or television channel.
- Famous meteorologists are few because it is a modern science. Toricelli, Ben Franklin, and Peterson are renowned in this field.
- The following meteorology ideas can be found in:

HUG A TREE

What Makes a Perfect Day?
Make a Rainbow
Measure the Wind
Snowjob
Measure Shadows
How Deep is Your Snowdrift?
The Seasons Go Round and Round
Quiet Time
What Color Is Spring?
Make a Snowflake

MUDPIES TO MAGNETS

Rainbow in a Jar
Lightning and Thunder, Wow It's Scary
Mushy, Slushy, Melty Snow
Weather or Not I Should Wear It
What's the Color of the Day
Rainbow Rain
Rainbow Stew
Weather Art
Put the Sunny Side Up
Drying Race
Egg Carton Rainbows
Thermometer Play
Raincycle
Keep It Cool
Shirts in the Sun
Puddle Walk
Rain Measures
Marching of the Seasons
Weather Predictors
Tornado in a Jar

COOL HAT FOR A HOT DAY

Language with science

soak
freeze
cold
melt
cool
hat
warm
sweat
long
time
fast
faster
short

Things you will need

a number of 9" x 9" (22 cm) square pieces of cotton material (torn sheets are great)

l large head-size bowl

water
wax paper
freezer
timer

Turn a hot, sultry day into an experiment. Cool off and have fun. Experiment with the sun! The shade! Run, get hotter, keep cooler with your cold hat. But don't take too long! Hey, that's important. Time. Keep track of time. What makes this activity science is collecting data. Play first, and then cool off. How much time did it take for your cooler to wear out?

What to do

1. Cut or tear 9" x 9" (22 cm) squares from a clean cotton sheet. Soak the cotton squares in water. Wring out the water. Place the squares on an overturned bowl, separating each with a sheet of wax paper. Make a stack of 8 to 10 squares. Place bowl in freezer.

2. When the hats are frozen, remove the bowl from the freezer. Let the children each take a hat off the bowl and place it on their heads.

3. How long does it take for your hat to melt? Do you think it's a cool way to cool off?

Want to do more?

Do the hats melt faster in the sun or in the shade? Are there other kinds of hats to help you stay cool? What else can you do to cool off on a hot day?

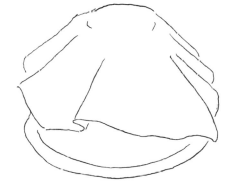

HOT AND COLD: THE BASICS

Language with science

hot/cold
water
wet/dry
feel
same/different
temperature

Things you will need

tub of hot water
tub of cold water
towels

The young child beginning to use and understand language receives many warnings. One of those warnings is "TOO HOT," but little meaning is attached to the concept until the child has experienced "HOT." This activity is a fun, safe, and controlled way to experience HOT and COLD. You will want to encourage the children to dry their own hands to develop a self-help skill too!

What to do

1. Place the two tubs together on a table easily reached by the children. (Remember — not TOO hot. You can add ice to the cold tub to increase the contrast of the temperature).

2. Encourage the children to put their hands into the tubs and discuss how they feel. What does the hot water make them think of? How about the cold water?

3. Have towels ready for the children to dry their hands.

Want to do more?

Have other objects that are hot and cold for the children to feel. Discuss hot and cold as you carry out daily activities, as in the bathroom or at lunch time. Older children can use a thermometer to test the water temperature. Have them put several containers of water in order by temperature, then check their accuracy with a thermometer.

ICE CUBE NECKLACES

Language with science

hot
sun
solar energy
shade
freeze
cool
color
direct sunlight
temperature
source

Things you will need

color-fast cotton yarn

water
flowers
leaves
collecting bags
freezer tray
water

Gosh, that sun's hot! What can we do to help us cool down on this hot day? This activity presents a way to help the children become aware of temperature differences in direct sunlight and in the shade, to realize the source of these temperatures, and, better yet, to discover a fun way to cool down.

What to do

1. Cut a length of color-fast colored cotton yarn for each necklace.

2. Have the children go on a collecting walk to gather pretty things to put in their ice cubes.

3. Place collected bits and pieces into a freezer tray and fill with water.

4. Arrange yarn so that each ice cube tray section has one piece of yarn submerged in the center of the water.

5. Place the tray in the freezer. Remove when frozen. Voila! You now have ice cube necklaces.

6. Wear them proudly as you cool down on a hot day.

7. Compare designs and colors. Watch as they melt. Wonder whose ice cube will fall off first? Last? Were your predictions right?

Want to do more?

Use colored water. Time the melting on different days and compare to the temperature that day. Place colored reflectors behind the necklace, i.e., aluminum foil, black cloth, white cloth, sponges. Does melting time change?

HOT BUBBLE FLIERS

Language with science

bubbles
warm
air
temperature
high
quickly
fast
lighter
cold
moves
replaces
float
rising
currents
breath

Things you will need

bubble mixture (1/3 cup Dawn dish soap, 1 cup water and 1 teaspoon of sugar)

container for mixture
bubble blowers

Bubbles, bubbles, love to make bubbles, just any excuse to blow bubbles. What's that you say? Outside on a cold winter day to blow bubbles? Yes! Grab a bottle of warmed bubble solution, take your warm breath, and out you go to send hot air bubbles up into the cold sky.

Cold air is heavier than warm air. Air rises as it gets warm and cold air moves in to take its place. This causes currents of air to move around inside as well as out of doors. To show how this happens, we use warmed bubble solution and our own warm body air. The bubbles we blow on a cold winter day will float upward as the warm air inside rises.

What to do

1. Let children mix bubble mixture indoors.

2. Go outside on a cold winter day and let them blow bubbles.

3. Observe the bubbles as they float upward.

4. Explain that the child's warm breath makes the bubbles very light and that cold air is heavier than warm air.

5. Why do the bubbles fly up so quickly? How high will they fly? Watch and see.

Want to do more?

Try the same experiment using cold water, approximately the same temperature as the outdoor air. What happens? Compare the two types of Bubble Fliers. Experiment with various bubble blowers. Does the type you use make a difference?

SOLAR WARMER

Language with science

solar
dehydrate
melt
renewable
heat
energy
nonrenewable

Things you will need

marshmallows
chocolate squares
muffin tin

foil and paper
baking cups

The energy of the sun has heated our earth for billions of years. The potential of the sun as a source of energy to heat and light our homes and to perform various jobs for us has just begun to be evaluated. For the past 50 years industrial and business growth has been directly related to the fossil fuels, coal and oil. As these nonrenewable resources begin to deplete, we have looked to alternative energy sources to be substituted. Sun power or solar energy is one of those renewable resources that has found use. We can try to make it do some work for us.

Sunlight contains rays that we can and cannot use. The rays we cannot use are called ultraviolet; those we can use are called infrared. The ultraviolet rays darken our skins on hot summer days. Too much exposure to these rays will cause our skins to burn. Infrared rays can be used to warm and even, on very very hot days, to cook food. This activity shows us how solar energy can be used to prepare a delicious snack for ourselves.

PAPER

FOIL

What to do

1. Line 1/2 of muffin tin with foil baking cups.

2. Line 1/2 of muffin tin with paper baking cups.

3. Place 1 marshmallow in each cup — place 1 chocolate square on top of each marshmallow.

4. Place your solar warming muffin in direct sunlight.

5. Turn the warmer to face the sun as it crosses the sky.

6. Observe the ingredients. When the chocolate melts over the marshmallow, it's time to eat the treat. It might be messy but ooh, it's good!

7. Are the treats in paper ready before or after the treats in foil.

8. For larger groups — just place paper and foil cups on a cookie sheet and place in direct sunlight.

Want to do more?

Try the same procedure using strips of fruit. Dried fruit can be a nutritious treat for the children.

LET'S DEW IT

Language with science

dew
condense
water vapor
condensation

Things you will need

pint jars with lids
glass
cold water
towels
ice

When warm air comes into contact with cool surfaces on the ground or on a cold object such as a glass, it becomes cooled to its "dew" point. When this happens, we see moisture form on the surface of the glass or on the blades of grass. This is surface condensation, and is called dew. This activity will show you how to make and collect your own "dew." Choose a hot, humid day and let's dew it!

What to do

1. Place a glass where the children can easily see it. Add ice, then water to fill the glass.

NOTE: Be careful not to spill.

2. Begin talking about how water is found in the air, ask the children how they can tell if water is in the air. If the humidity is high and you have taken enough time, water should have condensed on the outside of the glasses.

3. How did the water get there? Did I spill some water? Then what happened if the water didn't spill. Someone might say that the water came from the air. Here is an experiment to show that it must have.

4. Fill a jar with ice cubes and add water to fill. Put the lid on tight! Wipe off with a towel so the jar is dry and does not leak.

5. After a few minutes, what do you see? The cold jar will sweat. Moisture condenses from the air onto the outside of the cold jar. Wipe off the cold jar and allow water to condense again. Turn the freshly dried jar over to demonstrate that it is not leaking.

6. Where does the water come from? Why everyone knows, it's from the air. Water vapor comes from the air and condenses on your cold glass.

Want to do more?

Evaporate the water from the container. Will the water evaporate if the lid is left on? Fill a jar with warm water. What happens? Place a cold piece of metal in the freezer. Put it out into humid air and watch water condense on the cold surface.

EVAPORATION PLUS

Language with science

evaporation
wind
solar heat
shade
dry
fast
slow
long
short

Things you will need

water

coffee can or margarine tub lids

medicine droppers — a request to parents will usually result in more than enough

Children have some experience with evaporation everyday. They get out of the tub with wet hair and a while later their hair is dry. They put paintings and clay creations in a special place to dry. When they paint outside with buckets of water and paintbrushes, the paintings disappear. Although young children cannot grasp the concept of changes in matter that occur in evaporation, they can, all by themselves, have a good time manipulating the variables that affect the process.

What to do

1. Following an experience such as painting with water, easel painting, or some other activity involving evaporation, talk with the children about where the water went. Encourage them to share their own ideas. Can they think of other times when water evaporates or goes into the air? You don't need to push the word "evaporation." Most children will understand the meaning as you use it in conversation. Active participation in experimenting and thinking is more important than learning a new science word. What are their ideas about how we could make water evaporate faster? Slower? Let's try out the ideas and see what happens.

2. Give the children one lid each. Have them put a few drops of water on the lids using the medicine droppers. With just a little water, things will happen faster. They can then put the lid where they think the water will evaporate quickly. The choice of placement is is up to each child.

3. Check on the water throughout the day. Where did the water evaporate the fastest? The slowest? Can the children draw any conclusions? A good way to approach this is to say, "If we wanted to make water evaporate in a hurry, where would be the best place to put it?" "If we wanted to keep our water for a long time, where do you think we should put it?" "Let's try it and see if we are right." Then — try it and see if you ARE right!

Want to do more?

Put a few drops of water on two pieces of construction paper. Take turns fanning one with a piece of cardboard. Leave the other one alone. What makes the water evaporate faster? In winter, put one lid of water by your heat source and one outside. Which one dries faster? What can you do to prevent evaporation?

DIZZY SNAKE

Warm air is lighter than cold air, so it rises as it gets warm and cold air moves in to take its place. This causes currents of rising air. Birds float upward on rising currents of hot air. Gliders, which are airplanes without motors, stay high up in the sky for many hours on warm days. The currents of warm air that help the birds and gliders fly are called thermals. A thermal gradient occurs whenever a continuous supply of hot air causes differences in air flow upward. A place to see this phenomena happen is over a black parking lot or a hot water heating device. No air is blown, just hot air is rising.

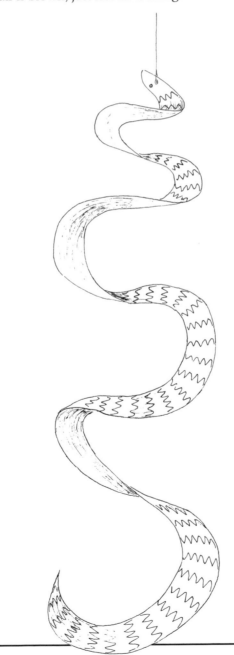

What to do

1. Draw a spiral on a square of paper.

2. Decorate the snake as you wish. Punch hole in center of snake's head with pencil.

3. Cut along the spiral line.

4. Hang the snake above a warm radiator using a piece of thread.

5. Observe the snake spin as the warm air rises.

6. Now hang your snake over the floor. What happens?

Want to do more?

Fix your snake on the sharpened end of a pencil. Place the eraser end of the pencil in some clay or a thread spool. Place directly on the radiator. Compare it to your hanging snake. Place it on the floor. Also compare it to your hanging snake. Provide additional paper for children to cut out more snakes.

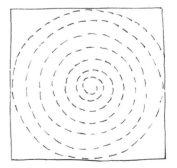

THE BIG MELT DOWN

Language with science

salt
solution
temperature
freeze
melt
melt more
faster
color
blue
red

Things you will need

1 paper cup per child

food coloring (red and blue)

very cold water

salt

ice on the sidewalk or ground.

This activity is best on a sunny day after a snow or ice storm.

The salt trucks are on the roads again. That means cold weather, freezing temperatures mixed with ice, sleet, or snow. What does the salt do? Does it melt the snow or ice? Not really. Sun or warm weather does the melting. The salt lowers the temperature at which water freezes. When the truck puts the salt on the road, then the termperature at which ice forms changes to -16 $^\circ$ C (4 $^\circ$ F). This means that the ice and snow stay in its liquid form longer and thus disappear from the road surface faster because it doesn't change back to ice as soon. However, when the temperature is very low, below -16 $^\circ$ C (4 $^\circ$ F), salt water freezes just like regular water. All of this freezing and melting at different temperatures is not what your four or five year olds need to understand. What they can observe is that salt has an effect on freezing of water, and that is the reason it is used on sidewalks and streets during bad winter weather.

What to do

1. Let children work in pairs. (Give each child one paper cup.)

2. Have them prepare a salt water solution in one cup — 2 tablespoons of salt to 1 cup. Then fill with water and stir. Add one drop of red food coloring to designate that this cup contains the salt solution.

3. Now fill the second cup with water. Add one drop of blue food coloring.

4. Have children dress warmly, then go outside with one child carrying the salt (red) solution and the other carrying the plain (blue) water.

5. Now they pour their cups onto the ice. We want to find out which one melts the most ice. Which one do you think will make the biggest hole? They can now return to the room and go back to check on this experiment later during the day.

6. After returning to their designated spot, they will observe that the salt solution has melted the ice. This is because salt water freezes at a lower temperature than ordinary water. In other words, it has to get colder than 32 $^\circ$ F (0 $^\circ$ C) before salt water will freeze.

Want to do more?

Do the same activity using a thermometer. Do "Tin Can Ice Cream" in HUG A TREE.

BLOW WIND BLOW

Language with science

blow
wind
force
air

Things you will need

fan
file folder

set of objects that
can be blown
around such as
   small pieces of
     paper
   feathers
   pieces of
     styrofoam cup
   small rubber
     ball
   leaves

The result of the movement of air is wind. Wind strength can be tested with an instrument called an anemometer. That machine is difficult to make and calibrate and is also expensive to purchase. Can a sense of wind power or speed be determined another way? Yes, it can! Try this simple activity and see.

What to do

1. Choose a very windy day to do this activity.

2. Discuss the effects of wind. Wind is moving air. The only way we know about air is when wind is blowing and we can see things move or feel the wind.

3. Demonstrate wind by blowing a piece of paper across the table. "Wind is moving air."

4. Now it is time to test wind.

5. Set up 4 tests (or fewer if you feel it is too much for the children).

   A. A fan,

   B. The wind outside on a clear spot you have selected where the wind blows strong,

   C. The table (for children blowing), and

   D. Another table to test homemade wind machines

6. Demonstrate each area. Put things in front of the fan, put some that can be blown and others that will not be blown. Show how to wave a file folder to make wind. Blow on some things that will blow and not be blown.

7. Have each child select 4-6 objects that she thinks the wind can blow.

8. Take the objects to each station and see if the blows them.

9. Compare the wind sources. Which is the strongest? Does strong mean blow long or blow hard?

Want to do more?

Read the book GILBERTO AND THE WIND by Marie Hall Ets. Order objects by their ability to be blown away. You now have a way to measure wind. Place these items in the windy spot. The object(s) left should indicate how strong the wind was at that time. Measure the objects' movement. What gets blown the farthest?

HOT AND COLD:
LET'S GET PRECISE

Language with science

thermometer
hot
hotter
hottest
cool
coolest
place
sun
sunlight
shade
temperature
warm
warmer
warmest

Things you will need

thermometers (4 or 5)

NOTE: You'll need to talk with children about thermometers. The longer the line, the hotter the temperature. See "Weather or Not I Should Wear It" and "Thermometer Play" in MUD-PIES TO MAG-NETS.

An acceptable, and even recommended procedure, with young children is to encourage them to develop guesses (inferences and predictions) before conducting a scientific procedure. It's good science and good learning practice. So, they make a mistake the first time and get nothing correct. A discussion of an idea and of a scientist's need to learn to estimate before experimenting identifies skills that are necessary for good science. Of course, retrying the experience can only lead to more accuracy and greater confidence in individual abilities. It's a must to try, but estimate first.

What to do

1. Take children out of doors. Observe the area around the school.

2. Ask which place they think is the hottest. Let the children choose.

3. Which place or spot do you think is the coolest? Again, let the children choose.

4. Place the thermometers on sites selected by the children, i.e., bare ground, grass, sandbox, slide, blacktop, concrete, swings, climbers, etc.

5. Wait 10 minutes.

6. Let's check our thermometers and see if you were right!

7. Which place was the hottest?

8. Let's choose some other places, but this time let's choose what we think is the coolest place.

9. Can we find some places that have the same temperature?

Want to do more?

How can you cool down a hot place? Measure something in the sun and record the temperature. Do it again when the spot is in the shade.

TORNADO TOWER

Language with science

tornado
clockwise
counterclockwise

Things you will need

2 sixteen ounce plastic soda bottles with lids

sharp knife
plastic film canister

food coloring

Can such a simple thing as starting a circular motion in a liquid cause such a tremendous difference in a procedure? Yes! it can! Just try this activity without that twist and you will see the difference. The result of this twist is a tornado shaped funnel as the water moves from one bottle to another. It should be pointed out that in "real life," the tornado is the center of a low pressure area and is always moving in a counterclockwise direction in the northern hemisphere. Can you make this tornado move in both directions? The bathtub will empty using the siphon system observed in the jars. Which direction does this water flow? Can you change direction of flow?

What to do

1. Fill 1 bottle with water and add a few drops of food coloring.

2. With a sharp knife, cut a round hole in each of the lids. The size of the hole will determine the time it takes for the water to drain.

3. Cut the bottom from the film canister about 1 cm from the bottom. You will have an open tube slightly shorter than a film canister.

4. Remove the plastic rings that are left around the necks of the bottles when the lids are removed.

5. Place the 2 lids in the film canister tube so they touch each other in the center. Screw on the 2 bottles. You can make this permanent by super gluing the connection.

6. Turn to place the full bottle on top. While holding the bottles tightly, rotate the system vigorously in a counterclockwise direction.

7. A whirlpool should form in the system that resembles the tornado's shape.

Want to do more?

Look at "Tornado in a Jar," MUDPIES TO MAGNETS. See "Sand Clock" in **Hodge Podge**. Try turning the system clockwise. Look at water flow in the bathroom sink and toilet. Make a giant Tornado Tower with 2 liter-size bottles.

YOU CAN DEW IT

Language with science

dew
condense
water vapor

Things you will need

pint jar
ice
salt
water
large funnel
kitchen spatula
measuring cup

In some coastal areas the dew is a major source of moisture. Dew is formed when moisture laden air comes into contact with cool objects. The dew forms into drops on the cool objects, dropping to the ground when enough condenses out and it is too heavy to remain on the leaf or rock. What are the best conditions for dew to form? It should be hot, humid days, little wind, and cool nights. Can you reproduce the dew conditions (not really), but you can collect dew and relate that to the humidity conditions. Here's how.

What to do

1. This lesson should follow "Let's Dew It."

2. Have a child fill up a pint jar with ice. Add 65 ml (1/4 cup) salt to the ice. Add a bit of water. Seal jar.

3. Place the jar in the funnel which has been placed in a larger container.

4. Set the timer for 20 to 30 minutes.

5. Every 10 minutes on the timer use the spatula to strip off the water. It will flow down into the funnel and collect in the jar below.

6. After 30 minutes and the spatula strippings, measure the water. Write that amount down.

7. Was this day a humid day? If it was the children should have collected more water than on a dry day. Keeping track of the water will tell you this.

Want to do more?

Evaporate the water from the container. Relate to hot sweaty days — something in their environment. When we run notice how hot and sweaty we are.

COBALT CLOWN, WILL IT RAIN?

Language with science

humidity
change
moisture
forecast

Things you will need

cutout of cobalt clown (enlarge to desired size)

cobalt chloride soaked piece of coffee filter

The chemical cobalt chloride is fairly easy to obtain from your local junior or senior high school. As a chemical, cobalt chloride, when left exposed to the air, absorbs or loses moisture. Changing of color occurs as the water is trapped in the crystals or lost back to the atmosphere. The more varied the humidity, the easier the change is to observe. If the crystals are evaporated on thin sheets of filter paper and dried slightly in an oven, the first change is quite evident.

What to do

1. Have each child cut out the clown picture and color it; the teacher tapes a piece of the cobalt chloride soaked filter paper in the eye spot. Children do not need the prolonged contact with the chemical.

2. Explain that the clown's eyes can tell if it is going to rain. They do this because the chemical in the paper on the eye changes color when there is more moisture in the air.

3. If the time chosen to create this humidity forecaster is one of dryness, then a simple spray from a mister will cause an immediate change. (Not too much or the color might run.)

4. Have the children observe the initial color of the clown's eyes. Explain how humidity affects the color. Leave several clown heads in the room. Send the rest home with the children. Place the clown face in a permanent spot and observe regularly. When it is about to rain, the eyes should become more blue. (This doesn't work well in an air conditioned room.)

Want to do more?

Find a barometer. It usually contains a device to determine humidity. See if a high humidity count agrees with the clown's eyes. Humidity is one way to determine if it will rain, are there others?

CUT OUT EYES,
TAPE IN FILTER
PAPER WHICH
HAS BEEN SOAKED
IN COBALT CHLORIDE.

WHAT IS HIDING IN THE AIR?

Language with science

air pollution
airborne particles
asthma
allergies

Things you will need

tissues or toilet paper

pushpins or thumbtacks

10 centimeter (4 in) square sheets of paper

clear petroleum jelly

tissue paper magnifier

The sky is full of all sorts of things that fly. Children notice the big ones: the planes, birds, kites, and such. They see tumbleweeds, leaves, and paper bags as the wind tosses them about on windy days. But even finer particles are present in the air. Smoke from burning leaves, exhaust from cars and factories, dust from fields and roads all gather in the air until gravity slowly filters them out. These particles are a part of our earth and our environment. Some will always be present, but others need not be. This activity does not focus on the pro or con of airborne particles. It just shows they are present. It's a good basic building block to begin to help children understand pollution and how it effects the quality of the air we breathe. That knowledge can go a long way in helping growing children make future decisions on the quality of our air.

What to do

1. Take the children for a short walk with a box of tissues or toilet paper.

2. Select various spots on the walk to test for evidence of dirt. Choose places that appear to be clean such as picnic table tops, rail tops, or large leaves of low growing shrubs or trees. Wipe across the surface of the objects. See what appears on the tissues.

3. Discuss where this material could have originated. Talk about air pollutants — dust, factory, or car exhausts. They must be in the air or our tissues would not have smudged. Let's find out if we have airborne particles where we live.

4. Return to the school and select 4-6 spots to run this experiment. Thumbtack down the 10 cm pieces of white paper at each location.

5. Cover the paper surface with a very thin layer of petroleum jelly.

6. Return to each spot daily. Remove one piece of paper each day to examine closely. Compare the amount of build up over time.

Want to do more?

Do a month long study. Check particulate count in different locations, especially near a dusty or heavily polluted spot. Read the paper and follow the news for cause and effect as it relates to your findings. See "Muddy, Muddy River" in the **Earth Explorations** chapter.

AERIAL ACROBATICS:
FLIGHT AND SPACE

AERIAL ACROBATICS: FLIGHT AND SPACE

Aerospace is

- the study of how and why objects fly in air and the study of flying, exploring, and living in space.
- studied by a variety of professions. Aeronautics is the name given to studying air flight. Aerospace engineers specialize in space-age theories about space travel. Astronauts are the outer space travelers that catch our imagination. Astronomers are trained in physics and geology to develop understandings of the world far beyond our solar system.

Ideas to share with children

- Aerospace experts build new airplanes and make old ones safe for us to fly. We go faster and farther on airplanes because they work everyday to improve flying.
- When you watch the evening weather and a far away news event, the information probably came to you by a satellite placed in orbit by the aerospace industry.
- Many of the products that we use in our cars, homes, and businesses were products of the attempts we have made to place humans in space. Teflon and plastics that appear in many things are examples of those successes.
- We hear of the successes of NASA, our government's aerospace organization, and are thrilled by the new voyages our spaceships make. Television pictures show the Space Shuttle going back and forth into space. Space stations to house humans are a reality. Space is the last real frontier, and it teases all of our fantasies.

Things to do

- Contact NASA; they have many educational packets and projects. Sometimes an astronaut or an aerospace educational expert can be booked to come to schools. Many major cities have an aerospace industry located nearby. These industries have speakers' bureaus that might provide experiences for kids.
- Visit an airport. Usually a company will find an airplane for the children to climb around and sit in for a pretend flight. Flights can even be arranged. Children are thrilled to see planes land and depart. A field trip to a major airport is an experience for all.
- Other aeronautics-oriented sources of excitement are model flying clubs, sky diver clubs, glider clubs, Air Force Bases, helicopter companies, parasailing, hang gliding, and ballooning. Most of these are watching not participating experiences, but the events can really enthuse children.
- Kite making and flying is another area to explore. Get your parents to help!
- Famous aerospace persons are: The Wright brothers, Billy Mitchell, Eddie Rickenbacker, Neal Armstrong, John Glenn, Amelia Earhart, Charles Lindbergh, Icarus and Daedalus Gagarin, Christa McAuliffe, Leonardo daVinci, Chappie James.

• The following Aerospace ideas can be found in:

HUG A TREE   Leaves Don't Fall the Same Way
                            Measure the Wind

MUDPIES TO MAGNETS   The Great Air Machine Race
                            Big Dipper, Little Dipper
                            Ticket to the Moon
                            Space Helmets

PARACHUTE DROP

Air is matter! It has weight and takes up space. The properties of air provide interesting opportunities for exploration. The parachute is a device that helps explore air and its ability to help us. A parachute can be shaped in many ways. Some are shaped like umbrellas, some are rectangular, others have special panels to allow the parachutists to steer them. As the parachute falls, air becomes trapped under the umbrella part and slows the fall. Without the trapped air, there is a crash landing. Start making parachutes and play with the design possibilities. Happy landing!

What to do

1. Let the children color or tie dye their fabric for a personal touch.

2. Attach four strings 10" (25 cm) in length to each corner of the 12" (30 cm) piece of fabric.

3. Tie spool, pine cone, or washer to the string ends.

4. Choose a place to drop the parachutes (a chair, a staircase, a climber).

5. Let the children drop their parachutes. Notice how long it takes for them to fall. What happens if a parachute doesn't unfold?

6. Take the children out of doors or into a large room. Let them take turns folding their parachutes and then throwing them up as high as they can into the sky. Talk about how the trapped air under the parachute makes it fall down to the earth slowly. (We don't want bumps on heads — supervise this activity closely.) Are there ways of folding and throwing the parachutes that work better than others?

Want to do more?

Try larger strings, cut holes in the parachutes, cut the fabric into different shapes — circles, triangles. Use different materials such as plastic or paper.

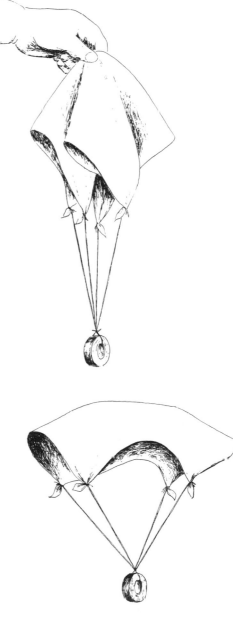

SPINNER HELICOPTERS

Language with science

fly
spin
helicopter
air
rotor
push
fall
descend
up
down
cut
fold
clip

Things you will need

paper
paper clip
scissors

drawing of model (see illustration)

Developed along the same lines as the rotary blade of the helicopter, this aircraft is really a glider whose two airfoils catch enough air to slow their descent. Given a source of power, they could climb up and fly away. Based on seeds whose natural structures produce similar effects, the spinner can gracefully circle to the ground giving children another glimpse at an attempt to mimic a natural event. Find an ash or maple seed and see the similarity.

What to do

1. Make the spinner as illustrated.

2. Hold it up as high as you can.

3. Drop it and watch it fall. What happens?

Want to do more?

Collect seeds from maple trees. Watch them as they fall. What's the biggest or smallest working spinner you can make? What happens when you add more paper clips? Can you make one from something besides paper?

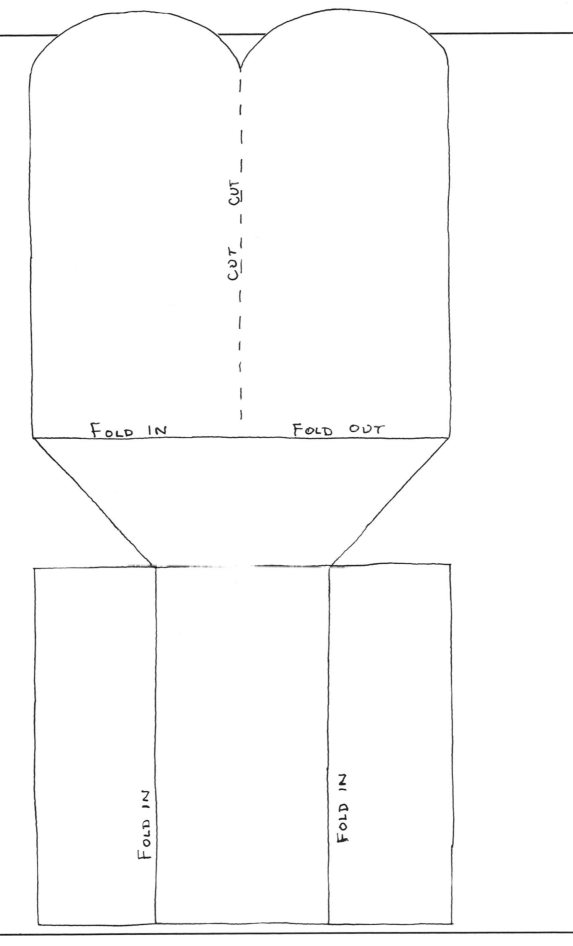

CUT CUT

FOLD IN   FOLD OUT

FOLD IN   FOLD IN

BLAST OFF:
PAPER ROCKETS

rocket
force
blow
reaction
flight
distance
launch

Things you will need

large plastic drinking straws

cellophane tape
paper
scissors

This rocket is one way to show the famous Third Law of Motion — for every action there is an equal and opposite reaction. This very important law was first discussed by Newton and remains as a foundation for modern physics. The law can be demonstrated in many ways. Here's one that's simple and familiar. A common occurence at any fast food restaurant when families receive their drinks is blowing paper wrappers off straws. This activity relates this common experience to the launching of a rocket. You can design rockets, launch them, and compare flight distances as well as in flight directions. Wow! What a blast!

What to do

1. Cut 4 strips from a 8 1/2 X 11 inch sheet of paper.

2. Fold in half.

3. Tape, leaving 1 inch untaped at the bottom.

4. Fold and tape to a point at the top.

5. Tear paper on untaped end to make fins.

6. Put the straw in the end that is not taped.

7. Now have the children blow on the straw, and their rockets will fly.

8. How far can your rocket fly? Compare flight distances.

9. Where did the power to make your rocket come from?

Want to do more?

Try to get your rocket to land in a designated recovery zone. Place boxes at various distances. Have the children aim and try to land their rockets in a designated box. Encourage children to create their own rocket designs.

STREAMERS

Language with science

wind
blow
flow
run
fast
slow
work

Things you will need

paper streamers
straws
stapler
fan

Moving air is called wind. Wind makes things move. What happens when the wind doesn't blow? Can we make our own wind? How? This activity shows how we can do the work of the wind ourselves. The power is in you. You can make the streamers fly through the air. Stop the power and they fall to the ground. Take your streamers and be like the pilot flying free, run and let it fly out in front or behind you. Stop running and see your streamer stop, hang, and be ready to go again.

What to do

1. Attach 4 paper streamers to each straw. Use a stapler to attach.

2. Have children hold the streamers in front of a fan. Observe how the wind blows them.

3. Go outside. Does the wind blow the streamers? What happens when the wind doesn't blow?

4. Let's run with our streamers.

5. What happens to the streamers when we run? Can you run fast enough to make your streamers fly straight behind?

6. How did we do the work of the wind?

Want to do more?

Follow a direction game. "Make circles with your streamers, make your streamers wiggle, make your streamers make circles around your arm." Have a streamer parade for a special occasion. Make materials available so children can make their own using the colors of your local school or favorite sports team. What can you do to keep your streamers from flying out behind you when you run?

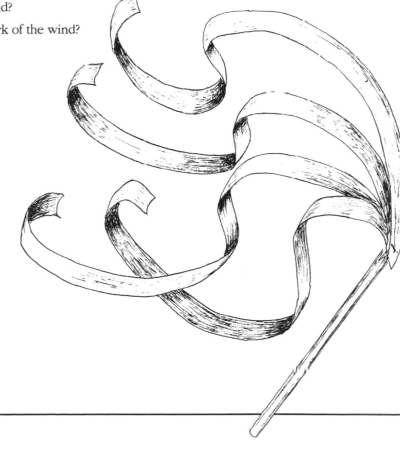

JUMPING ON AIR

Language with science

air
strong
fall
blow
tie
compressed air
jump
secure
pump

Things you will need

plastic produce bags from the grocery store

plastic-type ties

large garbage bags

The concept that air has volume and takes up space has a few traditional experiments that become too difficult or too boring for young children. This activity, however, demonstrates in an active, participatory, and fun way that air takes up space and, in fact, does work for us. When the children have caught the air, they can have the air catch them.

What to do

1. Blow up a plastic bag. Secure it with a tie. Let a child sit on it. What happens? It will pop or the air will eventually leak out.

2. Discuss the fact that one bag is not strong enough to hold us up. How can we make it stronger? By adding more bags and bunching them together. We can create a cushion of air that can support not only one child but many.

3. Let the children help to blow up numerous plastic produce bags from the grocery store. Use tie tops to secure tightly.

4. Place the inflated bags — many — into a large garbage bag. Secure the bag with a tie when it is stuffed with the air filled produce bags.

5. Let the children, one at a time, sit on, fall onto, or jump into the bags if you have 4 or 5 large bags.

6. What happens? Did the bags burst? Why not? The air distributed and formed a natural cushion for the children as they jump or fall. It's as strong as air.

Want to do more?

Compare as light as air to as strong as air.

AIR RESISTANCE RACE

Things you will need

timer

3' by 3' (1 meter square) piece of tagboard or cardboard (scale size of cardboard down or up to fit size of children)

Did you ever see a square airplane or a block-shaped racing car? No! They are sleek, slim, and aerodynamic. Even modern 18 wheelers on the highways have done everything they can to lose that blunt, square design that traps and holds the wind and slows them down. The race we are proposing is one designed to show that air resistance is present and is a factor even in such a simple thing as a running race. See you on the starting line.

What to do

1. Have the children line up single file. Designate a starting and an ending point.

2. On a signal, the first child runs to the marker and returns to tag the next child in the line. This procedure continues until all have run the course. The entire run is timed with a kitchen timer. How many minutes did it take for the entire class to run the relay? Record it.

3. Now repeat the entire process, only this time the runners must hold the 3' x 3' cardboard piece in front of them. Be sure the cardboard doesn't block the runner's vision.

4. Compare the times. Did the air pushing on the cardboard slow you down? Was there more air resistance with the cardboard or without it? Why?

Want to do more?

Repeat this procedure with larger pieces of cardboard. Try this on a windy day. Run against the wind, then with the wind.

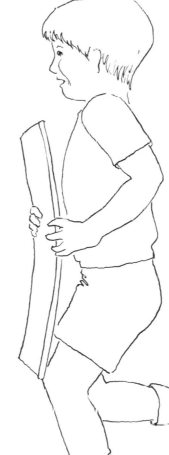

EASY KITING

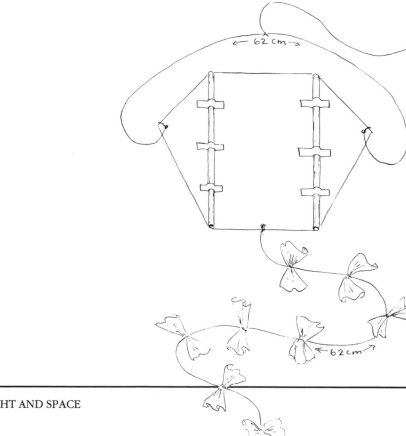

Language with science

fly
glide
lift
up
down
pattern

Things you will need

plastic bags
soft crayon
scissors
straws
tape
string
colored crepe
paper

Kites were the first flying machines. Gliders followed and, eventually, engine-powered aircraft. Children enjoy flying kites and learn quickly that kites will not fly unless there is wind. The stronger the wind the better. The wind pushes up on the kite's undersurface and keeps the kite airborne. Running with this machine that could leap into the air and stay for a time is wonderful. Construction of the kite will require a lot of adult help. Once it's made, the children can take over. Just try this easy to fly design and away we go.

What to do

1. Turn a bag over on its side. Lay the kite pattern (see illustration) on it and trace it with a soft crayon or permanent marker. Water color markers smear too much.

2. Cut out the kite. Attach the straws on the 20 cm cuts using scotch tape.

3. Cut a 62 cm piece of light kite string (the bridle), and tie it to the 2 points on the flaps through holes you have punched.

4. Attach the ball of kite string to the exact center of the bridle.

5. To make a tail, cut a 62 cm piece of string. Cut out 4 (seven centimeter square) pieces of crepe paper. Tie these on the string at 7 cm intervals.

6. Pick a windy day and go fly a kite.

Want to do more?

Bring in other kites to fly. Write to Estes Industries, Penrose, CO 81240 for kite information. Experiment with other things that fly.

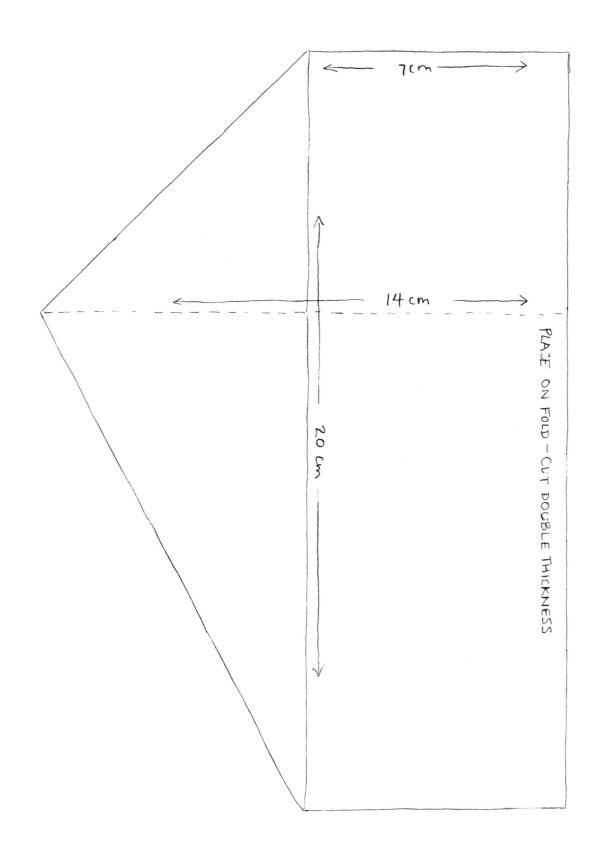

7cm

14 cm

20 cm

PLACE ON FOLD — CUT DOUBLE THICKNESS

THE AIR PRESSURE PUSHER MACHINE

Language with science

better
worse
best
some
use comparative terms

Length of string is important when comparing machines.

Things you will need

squeeze bottles of all kinds (honey, restaurant-type catsup and mustard)

scissors
various strings
baby powder

A machine is any object we make that does work for us. This machine does work when it pushes the string out of the nozzle and we use it for something. That makes it an automatic string dispenser. Or if we wish to knock a card over, it is a card-knocker-over. How does our machine work? It is an air pressure maker. When the bottle is full of air, it has normal pressure. When squeezed, the pressure is built up inside the bottle; the air must go someplace; it goes out of the bottle tip carrying the string along. Your machine is complete. You and air pressure are the energy that does the work.

What to do

1. Collect the squeeze bottles; catsup or mustard containers work great. Make a big knot at the end of the string. Thread the string into the lid of the squeeze bottle and tie a big knot on the other side. Put the cap back on and place the string in bottle. Test the squirter. If it doesn't work and squirt out the string, try another size string or enlarge the tip of the squirter opening to cut down friction. You might also use baby powder on the string to reduce friction.

2. Now place all the squirters out for the children to try. Which is best? Label each squirter with a word, letter, number, or color. Have the child try several and then verbally describe which is best, next best, worst of any three. What kind of string works best?

3. The objective here is to use descriptive and comparative verbal terms to tell why and how one is better than the other.

Want to do more?

Measure the length of string that blows out. Set up cards, dominoes, or toys to be knocked down. This is a tremendous hand muscle and perceptual motor skill developer. Have the children make up their own pushers.

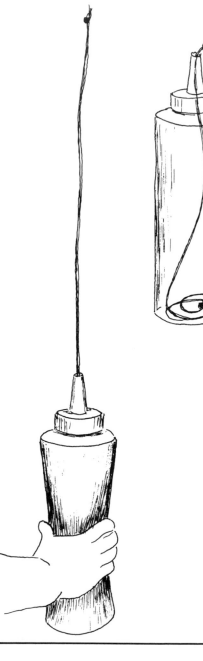

BALLOON FLIERS

Language with science

rockets
balloons
air
force
thrust
far
farthest
more
most,
gravity

Things you will need

balloons
paper clips

very light string
cut in 5 m (15 ft)
lengths

When we blow up a balloon and let it go, the air is discharged in one direction and produces a thrust that moves the balloon rapidly about the room. Other forces, gravity and friction, act to slow the balloon down. The long string will cause the balloon to slow down faster, but it provides a necessary tool to compare the amount of force released by the air escaping from each balloon.

What to do

1. Tie one end of a 5 m (15 ft) coil of string to a paper clip. Blow up the balloon and hold the opening tight. Clip the string to the balloon.

2. Let the children take turns letting their balloons blast off.

3. Where did it land? How far did it go? Compare distances by comparing the amount of string each one used. Make a graph. Why do some balloons travel farther than others?

Want to do more?

Use 3 different sized balloons. Which size balloon travels farthest?

FIRST FLIERS

Language with science

glide
glider
fold
softer
airfoil
wing
tail
fuselage

Things you will need

paper
scissors

Gliders are light airplanes that have no motors to move them through the air. When they fly they are towed up into the sky by a propellar driven airplane. When they are high enough, the glider is released from the tow plane. The glider then flies on the rising currents of warm air. The pilot flies from one warm current to the other and can travel many miles on a warm day. (See "Spiral Snake.") This activity lets the children make their own glider. It can be decorated as they wish. Watch the gentle glide that the plane makes as it drops from the sky. Children will discover for themselves that a smooth, careful launch results in a longer flight than a fast toss.

What to do

1. Cut and fold the glider as in the drawing.

2. To launch the glider, place your pointer finger in the "U" formed by the tail. Gently send the glider out into the air. It should glide to the ground.

3. It doesn't help to push the glider, just let it fall softly to the ground.

Want to do more?

Try other flying objects. Try modifying your glider by cutting it differently, or folding the tail and wings differently. What other kinds of gliders do you or the children know how to make?

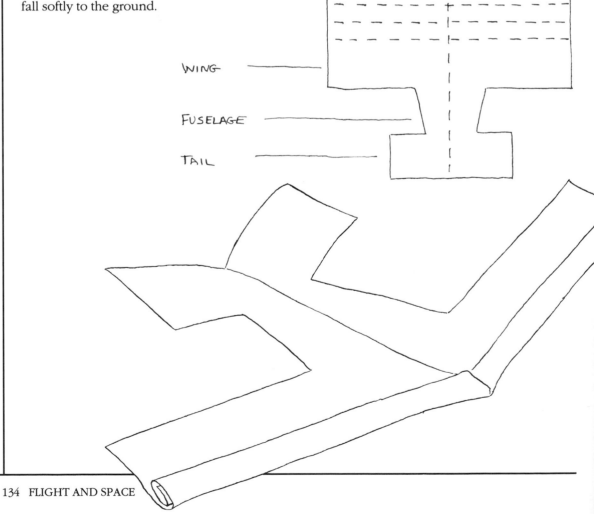

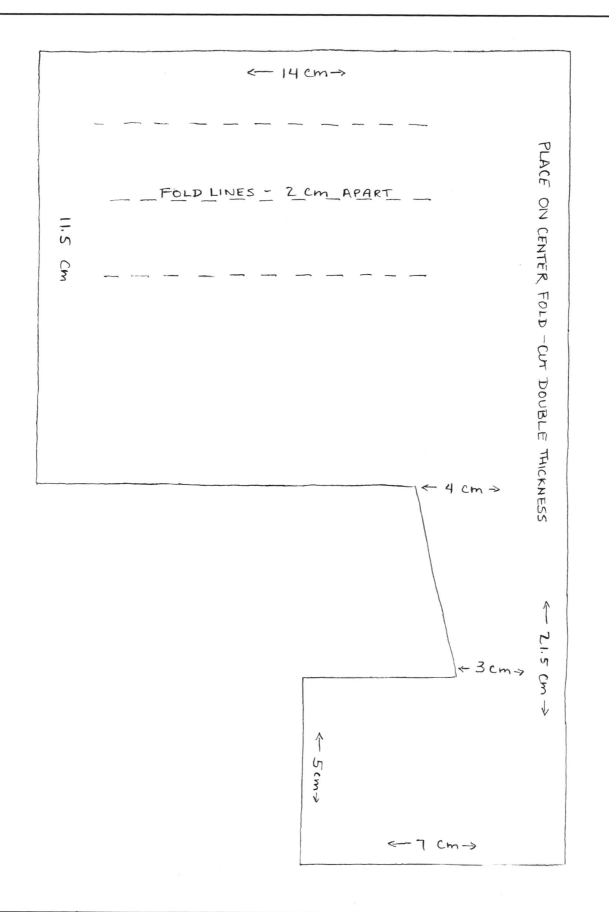

← 14 cm →

FOLD LINES – 2 cm APART

11.5 cm

PLACE ON CENTER FOLD – CUT DOUBLE THICKNESS

← 4 cm →

← 3 cm →

← 21.5 cm →

← 5 cm →

← 7 cm →

USAF MUDPIE STYROFOAM GLIDER

Language with science

fly
flight
glide
path
fuselage
wing
glider

Things you will need

razor blade or utility knife

paper clips

styrofoam meat or vegetable trays from the grocery store, use the lightest weight one you can. (Used meat trays may contain microorganisms.

To use, soak in a bleach solution overnight.)

Any simple aerodynamic form can provide young children with hours of fun and learning. With the help of the local grocery store meat or vegetable section, you can help to experiment with another flying object. This glider is easy to cut out and assemble. Experiment with paper clips on the nose to help balance the plane's flight. As with all flying objects, the key to an even and lengthy flight is an aerodynamic aircraft that is balanced to fly correctly. Get ready for take off!

What to do

1. Cut out the 2 shapes drawn on the next page. Trace the shapes on the styrofoam tray. Cut the design out of the trays with a razor blade. Cut out the fuselage slot. Place the wing in the fuselage. Center. Write the child's name on the plane.

2. Experiment with small paper clips on the nose until the best flight is obtained.

3. Head out into the yard or go to a high spot and let the gliders fly down, down, down.

Want to do more?

Compare different weights of trays to determine how it affects flight. Make a bigger glider. Does this affect flight? Experiment with the location and weight of paper clips.

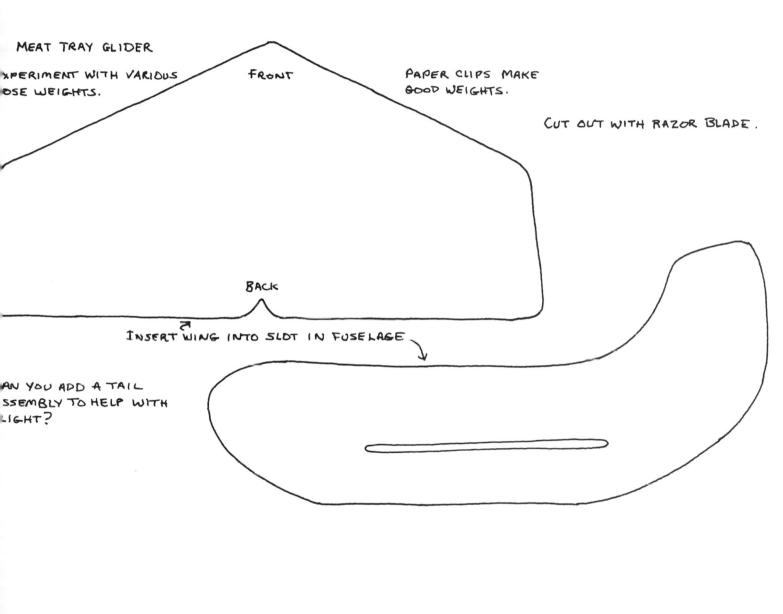

MEAT TRAY GLIDER

EXPERIMENT WITH VARIOUS
NOSE WEIGHTS.

FRONT

PAPER CLIPS MAKE
GOOD WEIGHTS.

CUT OUT WITH RAZOR BLADE.

BACK

INSERT WING INTO SLOT IN FUSELAGE

CAN YOU ADD A TAIL
ASSEMBLY TO HELP WITH
FLIGHT?

AERODYNAMIC FLIERS

Language with science

aircraft
airplane
glider
aerodynamics
streamline
shape
ball
faster
slower
wind
resistance

Things you will need

8 1/2 x 11 inch sheets of paper

paper clips

This swept back, jet version of the paper airplane can glide for long distances when folded properly and when the paper clip is placed in just the right position. The model introduces aerodynamics because it displays all the properties children see in jets, whether in the air or on television. The paper clip adds stability to the plane and brings a balance that keeps the plane flying through the air in the correct position. Take away these characteristics of aerodynamics and you lose the smooth, even flight. Try it. Then try your own variations.

What to do

1. Make a paper aircraft as follows:

   a. fold in half

   b. fold down corners on one end

   c. fold down again

   d. fold down a third time

   e. attach one or more paper clips

NOTE: You may want to use another design. Many are available in children's books. Another resource would be the children and their parents.

2. Take a piece of paper and throw it. How far did it go?

3. Throw the plane.

4. Observe which moves faster, which goes farther.

5. Compare the aerodynamic shape to the non-aerodynamic shape.

Want to do more?

Discuss aerodynamic shapes in automobile designs, boats, motorcycles, etc. Make a paper airplane collection.

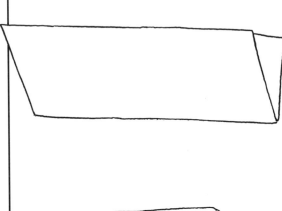

SATELLITE SIGNAL SENDER

Language with science

satellite
orbit
transmit
send
return
signal
reflect

Things you will need

egg cartons
popsicle sticks
film canisters
pipe cleaners
aluminum foil
string
glue
flashlight

The term "satellite" is used frequently, not only by those persons involved in aerospace technology but also by newscasters. Communication satellites are constantly utilized to relay radio, television, and teletype messages around the earth. We also use them to forecast weather and to watch people in other countries. This activity enables the children to learn about this highly technical instrument in a simple and fun way.

What to do

1. Use the egg carton as the body of the satellite. Have the children construct their own. Place a layer of aluminum foil, shiny side out, on the flat side of the carton.

2. When the individual satellites are finished, hang them from the ceiling with the aluminum foil side down.

3. Hand a child the flashlight. It should be one with a very concentrated beam. Have the child find her own satellite and shine the flashlight on it. The concentrated beam should be bounced back to the floor.

4. Repeat with each child. As you move to each child, talk about how satellites are used in communications, how television beams or radio signals are sent into space above the earth, and how the beam is reflected down to another spot. Aim is important. In real life, you wouldn't get the right signal if you aimed at the wrong satellite or sent your beam to the wrong target.

Want to do more?

Look at the spot where the beam reflects and try to guess where beams will reflect by the angle of each satellite. Read about satellites and how they are used. Refer to television news where people in faraway countries talk to each other using satellites.

foil

ROOTS AND SHOOTS:
ALL ABOUT PLANTS

ROOTS AND SHOOTS:
ALL ABOUT PLANTS

Botany is

- an area of biology that involves the study of plants. Plants are living things that reproduce their own kind, generally speaking, produce their own food with help from the sun, and don't move around.
- studying and working with all kinds of plants. The botanist studies the life cycles and processes of plants as well as their structure and classification.

Ideas to share with children

- Botanists have developed special areas of study. Several have helped to feed humans better and allowed our yards and gardens to be more beautiful. The horticulturist is a person who creates new plants to beautify our world. The agronomist is a botanist who focuses on working with agricultural plants.
- Plants provide many of the objects we use in our daily lives. Wood from plants is used for many of the furniture pieces in the childrens' homes. The houses that almost all of us live in are constructed all or partially of wood.
- Plants provide, either directly or indirectly, the basis for all of the food we eat. The source of the energy that plants use to create food comes from the sun. Try to find a food product that doesn't, in some way, come from green plants. You can't. The stuff in plants that makes them green and takes the sun's energy to produce food is called chlorophyll.

Things to do

- It is a wonderful experience for anyone to be able to grow a plant. The best thing for a young or old botanist to do is to grow plants. Take the children to visit a nursery or a greenhouse. Grow plants in as many different ways as you can.
- Collections of plant parts are always ways to involve children with plants. Collections can be made of fruit, nuts, thorns, bark, leaves, seeds, even roots. Which plants can you eat from the wild, which from the grocery store? From the garden or the farm? Try to show the children where the plants they eat originate. Spinach didn't just arrive in the grocery store, it had to grow somewhere.
- Plants provide the primary food source and shelter for most of our wild animals. The study of the relationships of living things to each other is ecology. Plants are a major part of studying about ecology. Look in the school yard. You will find the evidence of animals in the vicinity using nearly every plant.
- If you want to focus on botany for a while, bring the plant trowel, the potting soil, an apron, pots, a plant press, and some plant identification books. Then surround yourselves with plants of every description.

- Three famous botanists are George Washington Carver, Gregor Mendel and Barbara McClintock.
- The following botany ideas can be found in:

HUG A TREE

Spyglass Treasure Hunt
Hugging a Tree
A Wood Chip Garden
Everything is Connected
Touch Me, Feel Me, Know Me
The Texture Collector
Leaves Don't Fall the Same Way
Curve and Straights
Grow a Sock
What About Weeds
How Does Your Dandelion Grow
Seedbed in a Bag
Build a Plant Press

MUDPIES TO MAGNETS

Minimuseums
Oh, I Seed You
Seed Power
I've Got a Hunch, Seed
Color My Petals
Beat A Leaf
Weaving Nature's Colors
Beans in a Jar
Good and Juicy
Sprouts
Twig Race
Leaf Catchers
Outdoor Hunt and Find
Dance a Garden
Leaf Hunt Relay

COLOR AS YOU COOK:
OLD TIME EASTER EGG DYEING

Language with science

boil
cook
dye
natural

Things you will need

eggs
radish peels
onion skins
potato peelings
orange peelings

beet skins — just
a bit
cheesecloth
string

Most children who dye Easter eggs do so with dyes that are purchased from the grocery store. When their great-great grandparents were young, they didn't have access to such luxuries. This activity includes chemistry in both the cooking of the egg as well as in creating the natural colors that are used as dye. Natural dyes offer children a creative tool to develop a combined science and social science experience. Using vegetables and eggs from the grocery store allows the class to experiment with a variety of dyes or non-dyes, thus filling the Easter egg basket.

What to do

1. Place eggs and the peelings of your choice or combination of peelings in a cheesecloth bag, 3 or 4 eggs at a time will be fine. Tie the bag securely.

2. Cook the eggs — mix until hard boiled. After they are cooked, carefully remove the bags from the water.

3. After the eggs have cooled, let the children untie and unwrap the cheesecloth from the eggs. Observe the color of the eggs. This color has come from the natural pigment of the skins the children chose to use.

4. Try different combinations for new color creations.

Want to do more?

Dye cotton rags for weaving or collage making. What other things can you use to make dyes?

MAKE YOUR OWN GREENHOUSE

Language with science

sunlight
humidity
growth
greenhouse
estimate

Things you will need

clear plastic cup
potting soil
water
grass seed
cake pan

A greenhouse is designed to trap sunlight, heat, and water. The clear surface of the skin of the greenhouse allows light to pass through and warm the inside air, keeping the plants in tropical conditions year round. When adequate water is available, the high humidity adds to the factors that influence even faster and more luxuriant growth. You can create a large greenhouse to simulate an actual building by using plastic over a wooden frame, or you can use our mini-greenhouse set up. Your choice.

What to do

1. Plant grass seed in cake pan.

2. Water lightly. A spray bottle works well.

3. Place a clear plastic cup over a section of the tray. Place in sunlight.

4. Water lightly as needed.

5. Observe the growth.

6. Let the children estimate the height that they feel the grass in the greenhouse will be after five days.

7. Estimate the growth of the non-greenhouse grass.

8. Which do you think will grow fastest and highest?

9. Each time you measure the grass, ask the children to estimate how much more it will grow in another given time period.

Want to do more?

Visit the local nursery. Let the children see the plants. Talk with the owner about the plants and how they are cared for in a greenhouse. Plant other seeds in your greenhouse. Can the children figure out a way to make a bigger greenhouse? Let them try out their ideas, even those you don't think will work. They will learn from the process whether it works or not.

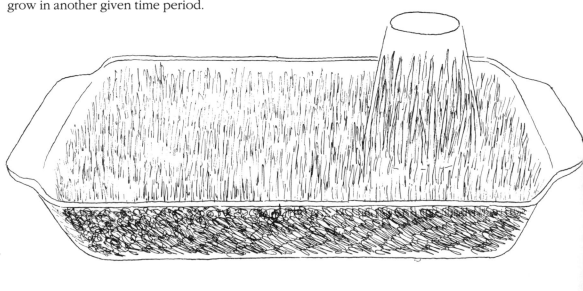

100% SUNBLOCK: WHERE DOES THE GREEN GO?

Language with science

experiment
plants
sunlight
survive
growth
grass
examine
underneath
over
on top of
recover
regrow
same
different

Things you will need

grass growing in the yard

a sheet of cardboard

How many of us have removed the wading pool from the lawn to find the grass all yellowed, faded, and pressed down. Through nature's work, the grass changes back to green, the spot fills in, and all those fantastic events go unnoticed. With a little attention, the cause and effect of the process can become an early lesson in the wonder of plants' relationship to the sun.

What to do

1. Place a piece of cardboard or a wood board over a patch of grass in the yard.

2. Leave the cover on for 3 to 5 days. This will depend on the sun and heat.

3. After 3 to 5 days, remove the cardboard and examine the grass underneath. (You can check periodically each day.)

4. What does it look like? Encourage the children to describe what they see. How is it different from the rest of the grass? How is it the same?

5. Observe the patch of yellowish grass and record how long it takes in days to recover and regrow after removing the cardboard.

Want to do more?

Try the same experiment using a piece of clear plastic. What happens? Why? Ask the children if they have a wading pool. What happens to the grass when you cover it with your pool for a few days? Put a plant in a dark closet for several days. What happens?

GREEN, RIPE, OR ROTTEN?

Language with science

ripe
green
ripen
rotten
spoiled
change
observe
seeds

Things you will need

green bananas
paper
crayons

Green, ripe or rotten? That is the question. How can we tell? Bananas provide us with an excellent model to study the phases of the aging of food.

What to do

1. Bring in some bananas and explain that we humans have learned to use some plants for our food, but that the original purpose for fruit was to reproduce or make new plants. Fruit helped do that by fertilizing the soil or attracting creatures that would carry it away. When a fruit ripens it is going through a natural process to help create more plants.

2. Imagine the bananas on a tree. First it is a flower, then it forms an immature fruit. It grows larger and changes until it is ready to form a new tree. What we are going to do is watch the bananas to record what happens as they ripen.

3. Place a bunch of green bananas in an appropriate place to ripen. Bananas ripen very fast in a brown paper bag. Have the children make a record by drawing a picture of one of the bananas each day.

4. Draw and color the green bananas. Peel one. Cut up the fruit. Observe, discuss characteristics, and taste the green fruit.

5. Continue to draw and color a picture of the fruit each day, as well as observing and tasting the inner portion.

6. Proceed until the fruit is overripe and spoiled. At what point do you stop tasting the fruit?

7. Have the children put their pictures in the correct sequence. They can be made into books or used for a sequencing game.

Want to do more?

Compare other fruits and vegetables as they ripen. Try to define overripe. Overripe is a cooking or eating term. Overripe bananas are fine in banana bread. Compare green tomatoes, ripe tomatoes, rotten tomatoes.

FLOWERS FOREVER

Language with science

flowers
collect
gather
choose
dry
arrange
preservatives
keep
last
florist
wildflowers
hunt
find
moisture

Things you will need

borax
white corn meal
jars or boxes
wildflowers
collecting bags
wire
florist tape

Children, like adults, want to give people something nice for a special occasion. Why not flowers? This activity involves the collection and the preservation of the flowers of summer. The preservation aspect involves a chemical change in which all the moisture is drawn from the flower, yet the color remains stable. The scientific term for this process is called desiccation or drying out. The colors of summer don't have to depart in the fall — they can stay.

What to do

1. Take children on a wildflower gathering walk. Let them gather a variety of wildflowers.

2. Mix 6 parts white corn meal to 1 part borax. Let children stir the mixture.

3. Fill bottom of a jar or box with part of the mix.

4. Place flowers in the jar upside down.

5. Cover the remaining part of the flowers with the rest of the mix.

6. Let the flowers sit for 2 weeks and them remove. (The flowers do not dry as quickly when the humidity is high).

7. Remove flowers from the jars. Let the children assemble their own flower arrangement. This may be easier to do if you replace the natural stems with wire and florist tape.

8. Now have children deliver the flowers to someone special as a special gift just for them. This activity would be very appropriate for fall and holiday gifts.

Want to do more?

Try the same activity with cultivated flowers. Do they dry as well? Which flowers are prettiest dried?

NOTE: Avoid use of thin, delicate flowers as they will not preserve as well. Use: Chrysanthemums, Queen Anne's Lace, Chicory (Cornflowers), Yarrow, Roses. Pick flowers at peak of blooming. Avoid wilted flowers.

IT WILL RISE
WHEN YOU YEAST EXPECT IT

Language with science

smell
odor
yeast
sugar
water
mix
stir
produce
feed
dissolve
bubbles
overflow
catch
measure
fungus
size
carbon dioxide

Things you will need

clear plastic glasses

dry yeast

warm water

sugar

spoons

plastic bowls or margarine containers

Yeast, a plant? I didn't know that. Yes, it is! It is a fungus, which means that yeast is one of the simple plants that reproduces asexually (without sex) in a form called budding. Yeast does not produce its own food as the green plants do, so it must obtain food from other sources. Yeast's food is sugar. As it eats sugar, two by-products are formed, alcohol and carbon dioxide (CO_2). When you make bread, it is the yeast eating sugar and producing carbon dioxide bubbles that causes the dough to rise. When you do this activity, you can see the bubbles of CO_2 form.

What to do

1. Give each child a plastic glass, a bowl, and a spoon.

2. The children should fill the glass 3/4 full with warm water. They then add one teaspoon of yeast to the water, followed by one teaspoon of sugar. Stir well.

3. Place the glass in a bowl to catch the eventual overflow.

4. Observe the solution. What is happening? The yeast begins to work as it feeds on the sugar. As it works, it produces bubbles and foam. As the yeast grows, it will overflow out of the glass into the bowl. It will form a one to one one-half inch head — much like a root beer float, before it spills into the bowl.

Want to do more?

What does the yeast need before it can grow? Try the same experiment without sugar. Will the yeast keep growing? Can you find other things to feed the yeast so it can grow? What do you think happens when we put yeast into the bread we bake? Bake bread with and without yeast.

HYDROPONICS

Language with science

hydroponics
growth
nutrients

Things you will need

clear plastic cups
cardboard
sprouted plants
cotton
liquid plant food
water

Hydroponics is the scientific process by which plants are grown in water without soil. The use of hydroponics has increased over the years. We eat bean and alfalfa sprouts that are grown this special way. Most zoos raise a significant part of their grass for herbivores in hydroponic growing houses. NASA plans to use hydroponics to feed space colonists when we develop space stations or cities on the moon. Hydroponics is truly a technology of the future.

What to do

1. Prepare a plant growth solution using the directions on the plant food label.

2. Cut out circles of cardboard or heavy paper that are slightly larger than the cup top. Punch out a 1 cm hole in the center of these (see picture). The cardboard supports the plant in water and slows evaporation.

3. Select plants to grow hydroponically. You can pull plants loose from the yard and wash the roots well. Or choose plants grown in the classroom. They should be about 10 cm (4 in) tall.

4. Wrap a piece of cotton around the stem of each plant and insert in the hole created in the cardboard lid. The cotton should hold the plant easily in the lid.

5. Add the plant growth solution to each glass and immediately place the plant roots in the liquid.

6. Place the plants in an area of subdued light, out of the hot direct sunlight. Treat them like any plant growing in soil.

7. Observe the roots and the plant growth. Replace the water/plant food solution as water evaporates.

Want to do more?

Leave some plants in soil; compare soil to hydroponic growth. Do traditional growing experiments using water grown plants. Take a cutting from a plant and root it in water. Compare its root growth to a similar cutting that is placed into soil.

ONE ROTTEN APPLE

Language with science

infect
infection
disease
germs
bacteria
contagious
spread

Following this activity, have the children dictate good health rules. Write them down as they say them. They may enjoy illustrating them. Post the list as a reminder.

Things you will need

a number of good apples

one rotten apple

toothpicks

stickers

Germs and infections run rampant in early childhood settings. The children as well as adults are exposed daily to germs that spread infection to others. Runny noses are everywhere. Cough! Cough! Sammy, Latanya, and Jose are absent. I am coming down with something. Please! I can't be out! Sarah was out for 2 days. "Nathan, wash your hands before you eat that apple!" I wonder how I can teach the children about germs and how infection is passed on to others. "Sally, please don't cough in Allen's face!"

Do you want to try to teach about how one organism can infect another? Try this one! It's especially helpful during chicken pox season!

What to do

1. Prepare apple slices as a snack for the children. Include a number of slices of rotten apple. Help the children notice the spoiled pieces of apple. Talk about infected apples and the diseases of apples, relating these to human sickness. Encourage the children to remember times when they've been sick. They were in the group, just like the pieces of apple were mixed in with the rest of the fruit. Recall times when several members of the class had the same illness. Speculate with the children about this. What do they think makes this happen?

2. Do you want to see how one bad apple affects the rest of the good apples? Let's do an experiment.

3. Place a "healthy" apple with each small group of children. Put a sticker on the apple to identify it. Explain that in order to infect an apple, it must come into contact with another apple that has the disease. Place a "sick" apple on the table in front of the children. Take a good look at it. Talk about what you see. Compare it to the "healthy" apple.

4. To infect the "healthy" apple, take a toothpick and place it in the "sick" apple. Then push the contaminated toothpick into the other apple. Put the good apples aside to incubate and allow the disease to grow.

5. In several days, cut the apple up to see how the disease has moved from one apple to the other apple to make it sick.

6. Relate this information to the movement of colds, flu, and other illnesses through the classroom. Discuss how a cold passes from one person to another through touching. Instead of a toothpick, a sick person's germs spread by touching with our hands, putting our mouths where someone else's mouth has been, or breathing in germs that fly through the air. That's why we don't share cups, we wash our hands before we eat, and we cover our mouths when we cough.

7. Cut up the apples and cut around the diseased portion. Discard that and use the healthy apple pieces for snacks or for other apple activities.

Want to do more?

See "Mold in a Jar" in this chapter. Wash toys together and talk about washing away germs.

4+ GROW A STEM

Language with science

seeds
reproduction
growth
roots

Things you will need

small plastic bags
paper towels
water
knife
whole potatoes
jade plant
African violet
begonia

spider plant or other plant that roots easily

Plants can be grown from parts of other plants. Many children are never exposed to this form of reproduction, as growth from seeds is the more common means of teaching children how plants grow. Humans have children, animals have offspring. New plants can be grown from various parts of parent plants. This activity shows how plants can be propagated from cuttings.

What to do

1. Display an example of each of the different ways plants can grow except by seeds. Be sure to label the method by which the plant reproduces.

2. Wet a paper towel. Fold it and place it in a plastic bag.

3. Cut a piece of potato containing an "eye." Place it in the bag.

4. Cut a piece of jade plant. Make sure it has two leaves.

5. Break a leaf from an African violet, a stem from a begonia, and a plantlet from a spider plant. Be sure to break the plants at a joint. Place the cuttings in bags.

6. Place the bags out of bright light in a warm place.

7. Observe the contents of the bags periodically. When roots are formed, place in potting soil.

Want to do more?

Try other plants such as strawberries, kalanchoe, coleus, or geranium. Vary the moisture and temperature. Does that affect growth? Place cuttings in a jar of water. Which method do you like best? Are there plants you can't get to reproduce in this way?

PROPAGATION

Things you will need

cleaned and washed milk cartons

potting soil
water
scissors
plastic wrap
peat
sand

clear plastic glasses

In the wild tropical jungles, many plants are unable to compete using traditional seed bearing reproduction. The jungle growth swallows up seeds by growing too fast for them or by rotting them in the wet, moist soil. Plants have developed other ways to reproduce called propagation. People have discovered these methods and have used them to speed up, short cut, or supplement seed planting. Many of us have experimented with propagation by recycling plant cuttings of flowers from relations or friends. This activity takes that casual effort and turns it into a real learning experience for children.

What to do
Follow the procedures on the chart to try the various methods of plant propagation.

Want to do more?
Visit a plant nursery or greenhouse. Bring in a parent who can show new or different forms of propagation or different plants to use.

PLANT PROPAGATION CROSS REFERENCE CHART

	STEM	LEAF	ROOT	TUBER	RUNNER	BULB
PROCEDURE	Mix 1/2 peat, 1/2 sand, fill milk carton 1/2 full. Punch hole in bottom. Water well. Cut stems into 5-10 cm sections. Remember which end was down. Make a diagonal cut on this end. Place stems into soil & put in sunny place.	**I.** Mix 1/2 peat, 1/2 sand. Pour plastic cup 1/2 full. Nick with razor the undersides of leaves. Wet sand-peat mix & push nicked portion of leaf in contact with soil, cover cup with plastic wrap. Set in warm sun. **II.** Mix 1/2 peat & 1/2 sand. Pour plastic cup 1/2 full water. Remove healthy leaf, cut small triangular piece with a vein ending at each point of triangle. Push triangle tip into soil mixture, leave one end out. Cover with plastic wrap, place in warm sunny spot.	**I.** Fill glass with water. Put toothpick in tuber so that the narrow end is down, the upper end will also be distinguished because you can see rudimentary eyes & buds. **II.** Cut 2.5 cm from a large fresh carrot, stand cut end in clear plastic glass. Cover to top of carrot with water. Keep in full sun.	Fill glass with water. Support potato with toothpicks so it is just immersed. Eyes of potato should face up.	Punch hole in bottom of milk carton, fill 1/4 full with potting soil. Lay in node where roots will be formed. Cover gently with more soil. Water. Place in warm sunny spot.	Punch hole in bottom of milk carton. Fill 1/2 full with potting soil. Put bulb in and cover to top of carton with potting soil. Put in warm spot.
WHY	When some succulents are broken & the broken end contacts the dirt, roots will sprout. This is particularly important for plants in a wet environment where seeds might rot.	Some plants have leaves that when broken off will begin new plants. These leaves are usually thick & succulent.	Roots are underground portions used to obtain water & food. Tap root in carrot. Sweet potato has clusters of roots.	Tubers are specially modified underground stems that store food and produce new plants each spring.	Trailing stems produce roots at nodes. When roots touch the ground the new plants are formed.	Swollen underground buds are formed to store food over dry times and winter.
EXAMPLES	Geranium Begonia Coleus	Begonia Geranium	Carrot Sweet potato	Potato Sunchoke Nut grass	Strawberry Ivy Spiderplant	Onion Garlic Tulip

THE AMAZING PLANT MAZE

Language with science

grow
sunlight
need
survive
seek
maze
water
phototropism

Things you will need

box with removable lid

dividers to place into the box

scissors

one green plant (preferably a vine plant)

water
masking tape

Tropism is the reaction of plants to a stimulus. In this experiment the plants are reacting to the stimulus of light; the response is called a phototropism. Plants need sunlight to live. They will seek out sunlight even when it's hard to find. This activity demonstrates that green plants need sunlight and will go to great lengths, twists and turns, to seek the light.

What to do

1. Cut round hole for sunlight to come in on one side of the box. Use masking tape to put two dividers into the box (see illustration).

2. Water and place the green plant in the box at the point farthest from the hole. Put the lid on the box.

3. Place the box with the hole side facing the sunlight.

4. Periodically open the box to water the plant and to observe how it has grown.

5. Observe weekly as the plant grows. What has the plant done to seek the light?

Want to do more?

Do the same activity, but cover the hole. What happens to the plant? The children can keep a record of what happens by drawing pictures of the plant throughout the experiment.

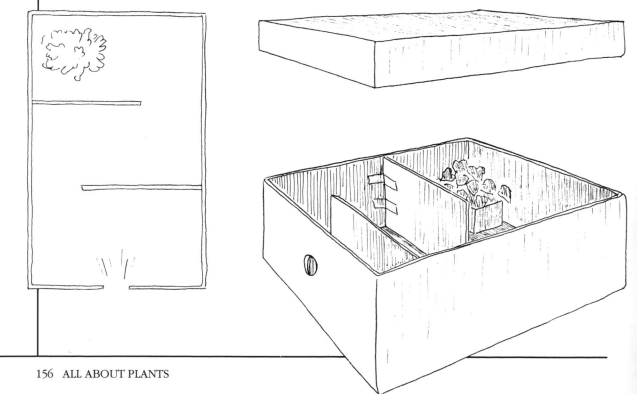

MOLD IN A JAR

Language with science

mold
grow
warm
dark
cold

Things you will need

jars with lids

slices of bread

apple
orange
banana
water
spray bottle of
water

Not all plants are big, green or grow in the sun. Some of our known plants are small and not very noticeable, yet they play a very important role as decomposers in the nature cycle. Mold is such a plant. It doesn't make its own food as green plants do. Children can explore how molds can appear and infect bread, living off it, using the food it cannot produce for itself. When you grow mold in this activity, remember that heat and humidity are the keys. Mold also grows best in the dark. The process is speeded up by allowing the children to handle the bread. Spores are in all dust so you should have a good growth. Just keep it moist.

What to do

1. Ask the children if anyone has seen mold at home. Also ask if anyone has heard the weather on television when the mold count is given. This explains how mold gets into bread. Mold spores are everywhere, they are very tiny and float easily through the air.

2. Pass the bread from hand to hand around the group. Drop it on the floor. Sprinkle the bread lightly with water.

3. Place the bread in the jar and close the lid tightly. Put pieces of fruit in the other jars.

4. Put the jars in a warm, dark place.

5. Every day or so check the mold jars. What does it look like on the bread? Is it different from the mold on the fruit? Are the molds different in color?

NOTE: Some children are very allergic to mold. Be sure they keep their distance. Obviously moldy food is not safe. Be sure children keep their hands off.

Want to do more?

Do the same experiment in the refrigerator. Compare how long it takes to grow mold in cold with the time it takes in warm, dark places. Why do we refrigerate food? Make a mold garden using a variety of foods. Use crackers and homemade breads. Many store-bought breads have preservatives. Add one piece of bread to the mold culture. Then place it in its own jar. Molds can infect unmoldy bread if contact is made. On one of your field trips, smell decaying leaves and compare them to the mold smell of this experiment.

UPSIDE DOWN PLANT

Language with science

geotropism
gravity
germinate
sprout
root
seed

stem and leaf
(cotyledon)

stimuli

Things you will need

bean or pea seeds

Ziploc baggies
for each child

paper towels
water
hanger line
clothespins

Do all plants grow the same way? Roots growing downward and leaves growing upward? What would happen if we turned it all around — like upside down? This activity will answer these questions as well as explain the reasons.

Plants respond to stimulus. One of those stimuli is gravity. A plant's response to gravity is called geotropism. Plants give off hormones in different parts of their bodies. Roots respond to gravity and grow down. A hormone (anxin) makes sure. Another hormone causes the leafy section to grow up. Turn the plant around and it will grow the correct direction. Don't believe me? Try it.

What to do

1. Make a seed bed in a bag by:

   A. Placing a towel in a bag.

   B. Wet the the towel with water, pour excess water out.

   C. Place the bean seeds in the bags to germinate. Watch them sprout.

2. A. Identify the root (white and it grows down).

   B. Identify the cotyledon (first leaf, it's green and grows up).

   C. Identify the seed as the food source until the green part begins to produce food.

3. Allow the plant to grow and lengthen to 3 to 4 cm.

4. Turn everything over so the plants are upside down.

5. Observe both the roots and stem (cotyledon) react to gravity by trying to turn around their growth. The plant can't right itself but it can grow a different way. Try several more turns and watch what happens.

Want to do more?

Measure the growth. Turn some bags a half turn to see their reaction to gravity. Cover one or two with a dark bag to see if they do the same without light.

MARIGOLDS:
LOOK AT SEEDS

Language with science

grow
growth
life cycle
seeds
plant
germinate
leaves
flower

Things you will need

marigold seeds
potting soil

dried marigolds that have completed the growth cycle

marigolds at various stages of growth

data sheet drawn on a large piece of paper

small cups or milk cartons to grow seeds

potting soil
glue

Marigolds, members of the dandelion family, seem to thrive in any circumstances and rapidly grow into beautiful flowering plants. The plants can be used to represent the entire plant cycle from seed to new seed, rather than to just grow seeds and send the young plant home to be replanted. Children need to observe the entire life cycle of living things and to observe change as it occurs to the organism over time. Change over time is a very difficult concept for young children to grasp. They lose interest in the slow, rather unspectacular issue of plants growing.

Let's see if we can add a bit of interest by bringing in stages of growth as we grow the plants. The comparison to actual stages as they happen, with a focus on recording the number of days the process requires, can go far in introducing the idea that plant growth is an on-going and time-consuming activity.

What to do

1. This activity should be done at mid-summer or when the marigolds are in the height of their bloom.

2. Collect or have available all stages of growth of the marigold.

3. Prepare potting soil and plant marigolds as you would at any other time. Use seeds purchased from a store, and show the children the marigold seed container, noting the seed characteristics and the picture of a mature flower.

4. Note the date of planting on a data sheet and glue several seeds on the sheet.

5. When the seeds have germinated and the children note the events on the data sheet, bring in a fresh marigold plant.

6. Discuss with the children that this plant has been growing and that their plants will go through the same steps in growth until they flower and die. When the flowers mature and dry, the seeds can be taken from them to replant, beginning the cycle again.

7. Cut off the flowers and buds of this plant so they will dry. After they dry the children place specimens on their data sheets. They are to note the days/dates this occurs.

8. Now plant your marigolds in a large planter outdoors to receive the sun they like. Water regularly, add a bit of plant food so they really grow, and observe the changes, adding information to the data sheet.

9. Send each child home with their marigold and an explanation of the experiment.

10. As the growth process continues and buds appear on the class plants, bring out the dried mature flowers. Show the children the dried flowers and the new buds. Relate that their flowers will mature and produce seeds, just like these dried ones have done. Save several dried flowers for the data sheet and allow the children to pull apart the rest to separate the seeds.

11. Compare them visually to the seeds from the original package glued on the data sheet. Ask what these seeds should do if they were planted. Plant a few to confirm their responses. They should grow.

12. Continue the activity until the plants have produced a few mature flowers which can be dried. The remaining marigolds can be allowed to mature without observing unless the children wish to follow through.

13. Review the data sheet and the life cycle of marigolds. Discuss the change and review the observable characteristics. It does take a long time for flowers to grow and grow old. But the change and schedule of events is predictable. With a group of 3 year olds, you know some will be around next year so you can repeat the lesson in the next season to reinforce and see what they have remembered.

Want to do more?

Compare our body growth to plant growth. Look at other flowers and try to relate what has been learned. Can you find the seeds? Observe seeds and discuss growth from them.

5+ LEFTOVER LUNCH

Language with science

leftovers
garbage
decompose
faster
slower
biodegradable
rot
mold
soil

Things you will need

soil collected from school yard or brought from children's homes — purchased potting soil has been sterilized and will not work as well

large flower pot

spoon

leftovers from each child's lunch — biogradable as well as non-biogradable items

Each day as we eat lunch, peelings, crumbs, as well as paper sacks, styrofoam cups, bottles, aluminum cans, cellophane wrappers, and fast food containers are left over. What happens to these leftovers? This activity will provide the opportunity to observe that food items decompose into a material that can serve as nutrients for plants. The children will also observe that litter that does not decompose serves no further purpose without recycling. This is an important bit of information for all of us.

What to do

1. Ask the children to save a fingertip-sized piece of food that is left over from lunch. Those children with no leftover food may save a piece of a sandwich bag or similar item. Make a list with the children's names and the item they contributed to the experiment.

NOTE: Don't use meat items. They might produce harmful microorganisms.

2. Have the children mix their leftovers into the soil. Pour the soil into the pot and add enough water to dampen thoroughly.

3. Place the pot in a storage area and water weekly.

4. After a month, let the children dig up the buried items. Can they find everything that was on the list they made? What do they think has happened?

5. Should items not be totally decomposed, rebury and wait another month. What has happened now? Remember that it is important to use small amounts of food as they will decompose faster.

Want to do more?

Try "Mold in a Jar" in this chapter and "The House of Worms" in the **Animal Adventures** chapter. Bring in a rotting log to show how things decompose in nature.

HOUSES FOR SNUGS, HIDEOUTS FOR HAMSTERS: ANIMAL ADVENTURES

HOUSES FOR SNUGS, HIDEOUTS FOR HAMSTERS: ANIMAL ADVENTURES

Zoology is

- a field of biology that involves the study of animals. Animals are living things that usually move freely within their environment and must obtain their food from other animals or plants.
- studying and working with animals. The zoologist wishes to determine animal life cycles, processes, and structures. Classification is important to the zoologist as is the study of the relationships that animals have to their environment and to plants and other animals (ecology).

Ideas to share with children

- Animals are an important part of human culture. Pets share human households. Cats and dogs, budgies, and goldfish share the love of children and adults. We are not a zoologist when we love our pets, but we can become one if we study our pet's habits.
- All animals have a life cycle that can be identified. Some animals are very similiar to humans, while others are different. All mammals have life cycles that are very similiar; they give birth to young alive, and they are warm-blooded. If children observe any mammal birth and life cyle, they can draw inferences about their own birth.
- Great diversity exists in the animal world. Children collect sea shells, starfish, insects, but rarely deal with them as animals. Humans are animals, too. Can you list characteristics that make animals, animals?

Things to do

- Every child should have the joy and responsibility of raising an animal, watching it grow, and bonding to that animal. Small mammals such as hamsters, gerbils, guinea pigs, mice, and white rats are easy to raise in the classroom and respond well to children's affection. Children should be able to check the animals out in a library-like system to take home for the weekend. Pet days and pet sharing are important zoology activities.
- A zoologist would "really" study an animal in depth. Studies on one of the animals could relate to food habits, nesting habits, or behavior. Collecting data for one of the animals offers a model to help future explorations. Attention should be made to the health of the animals. Animals all need food, water, a clean environment, and lots of love.
- All animals aren't big and warm-blooded. Make a list of all the animals that children can remember. Then look through books and magazines for more animals. Make an animal collage of pictures. Broaden their knowledge base for animal.
- You and the children can make collections of animal things or even animals. Collections of shells and skeletons of animals from the beach are good ones. Insect collection is a natural. You have to decide whether you want to capture and kill the insects or find them where they have died. Bird feathers are another easily collected item.

- Collecting an animal for a short time, studying it, and then turning it loose is a good model for young children. Discuss with them the importance of the zoologist studying animals and the responsibility for being kind and taking care of the animal before it is released in the same environment. Capturing a snake, frog, or lizard is an exciting event for little ones that can be crowned with scientific learning.
- Watching animals in their natural environment is a preferred method. While young children may not have the patience to study for long periods, nature walks with bird watching, log analysis, and associated journal and note taking introduce them to the activities of the naturalist.
- Supplies of identification books should be kept in the classroom for the teacher and the children to "look up" the strange new bird or insect that wanders by the school yard. Teach the child the name of a bird and it could be forgotten; but teach them how to find the name and identify the animal in a source book and you have given them a life skill.
- If you want to focus on zoology for a while, then surround the children with animals, collections, identification books, and animal cages. To dress like a zoologist, the white lab coat is necessary, as is a record book.
- Field trips can be taken to the local zoo, pet shop, farm, animal shelter, dairy, university zoology labs, or to homes to conduct a pet visit. Museums offer collections of animals. Walking field trips bring you into contact with local wild animals.
- Some famous zoologists are Rachel Carson, John Muir, Charles Darwin, Carolus Linnaeus, Anton van Leeuwenhoek, Pavlov, Watson and Crick, Jonas Salk, Louis Pasteur, Aristotle, Eugenie Clark, Diane Fossey, and Jane Goodall.
- The following zoology ideas can be found in:

HUG A TREE	Where Do Things Go At Night?
	Talking About Monsters
	Everything Is Connected
	Open House
	Follow That Critter
	Take a Bird to Lunch
	Hide and Seek for Critters and Kids
	Feed the Critters
	Creepy Crawler Race Track
	When is a Gnat not a Gnat
	Spring Is the time for Baby Birds
	Bites and Stings
MUDPIES TO MAGNETS	Minimuseum
	Pill Bug Palace
	Fish — Up Close and Personal
	Dinosaur Den
	Where Do You Hide a Dinosaur?
	Fingerprints: No Two Alike
	Body Game
	Listen to the Sounds of the Body
	My, How You Have Grown
	Bone Builders: Skeleton Creators
	Ant E Social
	Teeny, Tiny Tweezer Trek
	Your Own Animal Book
	Warble, Cheep or Tweet: Name That Tune
	Critter Cage

THE HOUSE OF WORMS

2+

Language with science

worm
bristles
legs
move
burrow
food
home
house

Things you will need

a tall narrow
olive or pickle jar

soil
water
black paper
rubberbands

small bits of grass

leaves
lettuce
coffee grounds

A worm is a very small animal that has no legs. It moves by using muscles and tiny bristles. Earthworms live in burrows in the soil and do not like daylight or robins. We can find them more easily at night in our backyards by using a flashlight and a fast hand. If we look for them during the day we must be prepared to dig in the soil with a shovel. During the daylight hours, the worms are in their homes in the ground. They only venture out when it's dark. If you're impatient, buy a supply from a bait shop.

What to do

1. Collect some earthworms.

2. Collect enough soil to fill the narrow jar.

3. Fill the jar with damp soil — be sure it's not too wet as this will drown the worms.

4. Place the worms in the soil.

5. Put bits of food (lettuce, grass, leaves, coffee grounds) into the jar on top of the soil.

6. Wrap the jar with black paper and secure with two rubber bands.

7. Remove the paper the next day to see how the worms have burrowed along the glass. Did they eat any food?

8. Keep for several days. Can you discover their favorite foods?

9. Release the worms in a safe place. Check in a while. How long does it take for them to burrow back into the ground?

Want to do more?

Discuss the food that worms live on. They live on organic matter (things that were once alive) like dead animals, insect parts, dead leaves, and other plant parts. Hold a worm and watch how it moves. Try moving like worms.

A HOUSE FOR SNUGS
(SHORT FOR SNAILS & SLUGS)

Language with science

slugs
snails
shell
movement
living conditions

Things you will need

large clear container such as an aquarium or large jar

a number of small sheets of clear plexiglass

slugs and snails collected from outside

rocks
sticks
grass
leaves
water

Slugs and snails are common land dwelling univalve mollusks. They are shellfish having only one shell. The slug has its shell reduced so that it appears not to have one, but it is related to the snail. Often times we see the snail closed and pulled back into the shell. This occurs when conditions are not correct for it to live. Snails and slugs can make nice pets if we create a home that has perfect living conditions and an adequate food supply. This activity lets the children create a home for these pets. It also allows them to study the animals' unique characteristics, their movements, and food preferences.

What to do

1. Put an inch or so of soil in the bottom of the container. Add some rocks, sticks, leaves, and grass. Add a small amount of water. It should be damp, not wet.

2. Collect SNUGS and place them in the SNUG house.

3. If you have fixed the SNUG house so that it is SNUG perfect, then the critters will come out and crawl around. Some will climb the glass and be observed. Now is the time for your children to study them.

4. Place an active snail or slug on a piece of clear plexiglass. Wait for it to crawl. Pick up the plexiglass and observe the snail or slug as it moves about. Observe from above and below.

5. Ask the children to describe what the movement looks like. Compare one snail's movement to another. Compare snails and slugs.

Want to do more?

Use a crayon to draw the snail's path. Put a cup of warm water under the plate. What does the snail do? Try to see what snails or slugs like by putting different foods in their house. Can the children move to slow music like snails and slugs? Can they curl their bodies like a snail shell? Bring in other shells to examine.

COOL OFF A FLY

Language with science

fly
temperature
hot
cold
environment
respond
lower
raise
decrease
increase
warm-blooded
cold-blooded
behavior
capture
catch
free

Things you will need

collecting jars
with lids (see
Hodge Podge)

ice
cake pan
flies

Do temperature changes affect insects? Is their behavior any different when it's hot or when it's cold? This activity lets the children observe the behavior of the fly when it is exposed to extreme changes in temperature. By observing the fly's behavior in both a hot and cold environment, the children can discuss what they think causes the differences in behavior. The fly is a cold-blooded animal. It is slow and groggy in the cold — but oh watch what happens when the temperature begins to climb.

What to do

1. Collect some flies in a jar.

2. Observe and discuss their behavior at the time they are captured. (This actually establishes a baseline for the behavior.)

3. Place the jar in a container of ice cubes or in the refrigerator for about 15 minutes.

4. Remove jar from cold and observe the behavior of the flies after their environment has been cooled. Are the flies' activities and behavior any different?

5. Put cold jar on window sill exposed to the sun.

6. Observe the behavior of the flies as the jar warms.

7. What do you think causes this change in the flies' behavior?

Want to do more?

Collect other kinds of insects, i.e., fireflies, ants, etc., and repeat the activity.

HAMSTER HIDEOUT

Language with science

preference
select
selection
nesting
behavior
hamster

Things you will need

hamster
hamster cage

pieces of material and paper cut to the same size and counted — cloth, tissue paper, kleenex, cardboard, paper tubes, paper towels, etc.

It's always nice to have a special place where you can curl up to take a nap. Hamsters like a special place, too. Will hamsters make a nest of anything, or are there some things they like better than others? This activity shows the children how the animals prepare their nests and just how particular they are about it.

What to do

1. Clean the hamster's cage. Place the feeder and water bottles back.

2. Place all the counted samples in separate piles in the cage.

3. Return hamster to the cage.

4. Observe the hamster's behavior. Record the items in order of use. After a time, count the numbers in each pile. Record this information. Hamsters are nocturnal animals. You will probably see a big change when you return to the cage the next day.

5. What does the hamster seem to like best? Are there things it didn't use at all? Try some other items. Can you learn how to keep your pet happy by giving it its favorite nesting materials each time you clean the cage?

Want to do more?

Offer the hamster a selection of food. Try the same experiment with a gerbil, with different hamsters. Are the choices the same or different?

RUBBER EGGS

Language with science

dissolve
float
vinegar
calcium
yolk
hard
soft
flexible

Things you will need

white vinegar
raw eggs

large clear glass
jar

This experiment shows the chemical change that occurs when vinegar, an acid, reacts with calcium carbonate in the egg shell. The acid finally will change or remove into the solution all the hard calcium, leaving only a soft shell. You can watch the process happening, because you will see bubbles form on the egg surface. This is carbon dioxide (CO_2), a byproduct of the chemical reaction. These bubbbles of carbon dioxide will even do work by lifting the egg to the surface of the vinegar. The carbon dioxide will escape into the air at the surface and the egg will sink. The process takes about a day. Check the egg for hardness before the children go home and again the next day. You might also note that the size of the egg is larger without the hard shell. The egg absorbs vinegar and gets bigger.

What to do

1. Show how an egg can be cracked to remove the yolk and white. Place the egg shell and egg in a container for the children to touch and observe.

2. Write down the words used by the children. Hard, snaps, breaks, white, etc. Add to their information that the material in the egg shell is calcium. Calcium is the substance that makes many things in nature hard. Another thing that contains calcium is our bones.

3. This experiment shows a chemical way to remove calcium from the egg shell without breaking the shell. Let's experiment.

4. Place an egg in a clear jar and cover it with vinegar. Use one that is deep enough to allow the egg to float and sink.

5. Check the egg periodically. Watch it rise and fall. Touch the shell for changes. It will become soft enough that you can actually bounce it. When it finally becomes almost see through, don't risk a bounce. We did and...

6. Look at your original list of words describing the egg and shell. Which words still apply and which don't?

Want to do more?

See "The Dunking Raisins" in MUDPIES TO MAGNETS. Try this with a chicken bone. It takes much longer. When it is soft you can tie the bone in a knot.

INVERTEBRATE SAFARI

Language with science

invertebrate
vertebrate
animals
classification
backbones
spine
zoo
yard
earthworms
sow bugs
millipedes
centipedes
slugs
ants
safari

Things you will need

collecting jar or bag

logs or pieces of wood in the back yard

clear plastic vials or film canisters

magnifier

Invertebrates are a classification of animals that have no backbones. Animals such as earthworms, sow bugs, spiders, millipedes, centipedes, slugs, and ants all fall into this classification. Human beings are vertebrates. We have backbones. The children will have a good time talking about the vertebrates going on a safari to find invertebrates. Play with the words. The children who enjoy using them will play along with you.

What to do

1. Go into the backyard. Carefully move a board or a log that has been on the ground for some time. What do you see?

2. If you act quickly, you may be able to capture some of these animals before they run away.

3. Move from place to place where there is tight ground cover, i.e., garbage cans, rocks.

4. Take the collected animals and look at them. Use a magnifier if you wish. What do they have in common? Where do they get their food? (Decaying wood and leaves) If you want the children to really observe their findings, carry along clear plastic vials or clear film canisters. Place one invertebrate in each container and pass around for observation. Plastic boxes with a magnifier in the lid are available through school supply catalogs. They are much easier for young children to use than hand held magnifiers. They also protect the creatures from too much handling.

CAUTION: Black widow spiders frequent DRY logs and brush piles. For safety sake, the teacher should turn dry brush over first. This is not a problem with damp wood. Spiders frequent dry spots.

5. Return the animals to their homes after this activity is completed.

Want to do more?

Explore the recycling of a log. Find one, break it open and examine the things that you can find, i.e., mosses, lichens, decayed wood, soil. See "Pill Bug Palace" in MUDPIES TO MAGNETS.

EARTHWORM GRAND PRIX

First, the collection of the worms; next, the big race; and, finally, returning the worm participants back to their original habitat. A wriggly adventure that is fun for everyone!

Language with science

earthworms
move
mobility
race
fast
faster
fastest
circle
winner
outside
shady

Things you will need

shovels

soil to dig up worms

shady outdoor area

What to do

1. Collect earthworms. An adult or older child can turn over several shovelsful of damp earth to expose the worms. The children can then break the soil apart to find the worms. Keep them in a container with damp, not wet, soil.

2. With a stick scratch a circle (1 ft/30 cm) in diameter into hard ground, preferably in a shaded area.

3. Put worms into the center of the circle.

4. The first worm to crawl out of the circle is the winner.

5. After the race bury the worms back into the soil.

Want to do more?

Do the same race using snails or sow bugs on a plexiglass surface. Notice the slime trail that is used for lubricating the surface. See "A House for Snugs" in this chapter. What other interesting things do you find in your search for worms? Do you find more worms in one spot than another? Wonder why? Put the worms in a plastic shoe box with a damp paper towel on one side. Keep the rest dry. Where do the worms go?

COMPARE ME TO THEM, ANIMALS

Language with science

similar
different
compare
same
like

Things you will need

large copy of chart
real animals

animal pictures and models

One of the ways to encourage children to explore their world and to use scientific procedures is to incorporate them into a study of their own bodies. This activity does just that. First, the children describe certain characteristics about themselves, then they compare these to other animals. The teacher or other adult serves as the recorder and gatherer of information. Each of the animals should be physically examined, and comparisons drawn as the observations are made. Remember, children cannot keep a bunch of characteristics in their heads, so take things one at time.

What to do

1. Transfer the chart in the illustration to a large chart or blackboard.

2. Discuss the characteristics listed for the children. You may want to go through and create a "this is me" poster for each child. Discuss the differences between children, and compare to adults.

3. Choose an animal and go through the observations, writing down the childrens' comments. Discuss the variations that occur in each animal.

4. When the chart is finished, over a period of several days, try to summarize similarities and differences that exist among animal forms. Use the descriptive words your children have used as you talk about the comparisons.

Want to do more?

Bring in new animals to observe. Try doing it with pictures and compare descriptive data. Visit a farm, zoo, or animal shelter and make observations and comparisons.

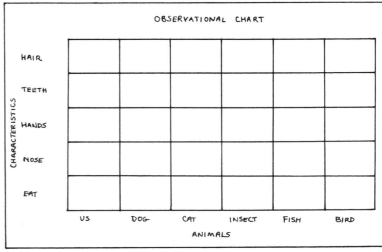

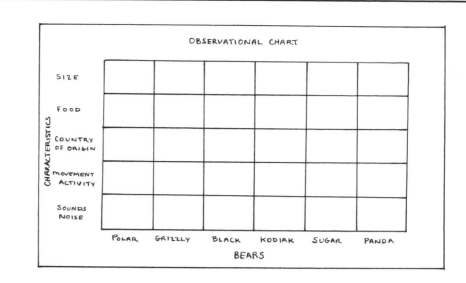

OBSERVATIONAL CHART

CHARACTERISTICS	POLAR	GRIZZLY	BLACK	KODIAK	SUGAR	PANDA
SIZE						
FOOD						
COUNTRY OF ORIGIN						
MOVEMENT ACTIVITY						
SOUNDS NOISE						

BEARS

THUMBS UP

Language with science

thumb
grasp
adapt

Things you will need

masking tape
peanuts
tangerines

When one begins to look at animal behavior, it is easy to evaluate such things as hot, cold, moisture, or other specific reactions of animals to stimuli. Classrooms can look at the ability of rats and mice to solve problems or train mealworms to crawl through a maze. One specific attribute, however, that has allowed humans to develop and evolve so highly is their thumbs. Do we take thumbs for granted? I'm afraid we do! How good is a thumb? Let's see!

What to do

1. Give each child a peanut to shell and eat.

2. Have the children describe the process.

3. Point to the cooperation that goes on between the hands and the mouth to accomplish this.

4. Have one of the children go through and describe the steps used.

5. There is one part of our body that we often take for granted. It's the part in our hands that makes us different from most other animals. What's that? Well, look at your hand and think about animal feet and see if you can figure it out. Yes, animals paws don't have a thumb. Your dog or kitty eats the way it does because it cannot pick up its food. A thumb is very important. Let's see what it is like without a pair of thumbs.

6. Tape the children's thumbs to their palms.

7. Hand out more peanuts. Maybe a few easy to peel tangerines. Let nature and frustration begin. What did you discover?

NOTE: Very young children may choke on peanuts. Use another food for them.

Want to do more?

Have a peanut shelling race. Try the techniques animals might have developed to make up for not having a thumb. Make peanut butter in a blender.

THE NEW SHELL GAME

matchings of the shells should be accompanied by a discussion of why they match and how the big one and little one are alike and different

Things you will need

sets of shells (one big one and one little one of the same kind)

Seashells. Most people have access to them, and children are fascinated with them. Shells can be used to teach many skills. Studying attributes of objects such as shells brings a variety and interest that cannot be produced by tokens or picture cards. Making comparisons by matching the attributes "big" and "little" is what this shell game is all about. Remember, it's not big-to-big or little-to-little matching, it's the big shape-to-little shape shell match that's crucial here. Now mix up those shells and give this new version of the old shell game a try.

What to do

1. Make up a shell collection with pairs of shells. One shell should be bigger than the other. Have at least 5 pairs of shells.

2. Hand the shell collection to the child. Tell them to match the ones that are the same shells. Tell them one shell will be big and one will be little, but of the same kind.

3. When the matching has been completed, ask the child to explain why each match has been made.

Want to do more?

See "Pair Up With Science" in the **Mathworks** chapter. Play the game with other pairs such as leaves, sticks, or rocks. Make a pair museum with the children contributing their own pairs of objects.

NO BONES ABOUT IT

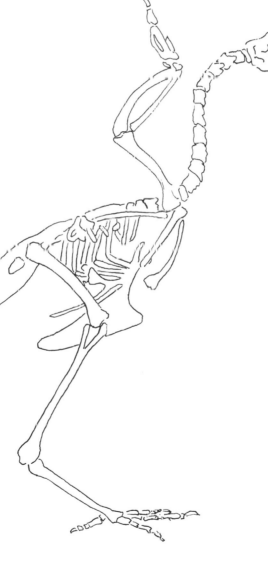

Language with science

skeleton
attribute
bone
structure
body
similar
human
chicken
animal

Things you will need

chicken bones
(boil and pick
the meat from
bones, let dry
place in Ziploc
bag; preference
given to neck,
wing, back, rib,
and leg bones)

drawings of the
human skeleton
and chicken
skeleton

pictures of a
human body and
a chicken body

The next time you have chicken for dinner don't throw those bones away. They have another use. No, it is not to feed the dog! It is to learn about skeletal structure and how it is related to the children's own body structures.

Chicken bones provide a tool for comparative anatomy with even the youngest child. Because almost all of us eat chicken, we are aware that bones are found within the meat. But what do those bones do? They are the skeleton that gives us form and holds us up. The bones in the chicken have comparable bones in our body. Can you find the chicken's neck bones? Where are your neck bones? Leg bones?

What to do

1. Have children bring clean and dried chicken bones from home in Ziploc plastic bags. Urge the parents to send in the bones mentioned above.

2. Ask the children to identify the chicken bones.

3. Compare the identified bones to those bones of the children. Yes, that is the neck bone of the chicken. Where is your neck bone? How is your neck like a chicken's? What do they have in common? Use the same proceedure for the leg, wing, back, and rib bones.

4. Show a drawing of the human skeleton and then a drawing of a chicken skeleton. Also, show a picture of a human body and of a chicken body. Observe how the bone arrangement is related to overall body structure.

Want to do more?

Have the children match the bones. Leg to leg, etc. Make size comparisons. Did your chicken have a bigger or smaller leg than your friend's chicken?

HOW MUCH, HOW FAR, HOW MANY: MATHWORKS

HOW MUCH, HOW FAR, HOW MANY: MATHWORKS

Mathematics is

- basically, the study of numbers. Measurement allows mathematics to define properties and dimensions and serves as the communication tool for all of science. Mathematics allows problem solving, abstraction, and generalizations to occur in their most complex form.
- is studied by persons called mathematicians. They manipulate numbers and explore complex multidimensional shapes. Much of their work is done in conjunction with other science areas. The Greek word mathema means learning. Mathematics has served as the vehicle for much of the highest form of learning in history. Early work was accomplished on paper or on the blackboard. The tool of the mathematican has now become the computer.

Ideas to share with children

- Mathematics is more than numbers or arithmetic. Mathematics is a way of thinking that includes problem solving and logic. We can develop tasks that allow children practice in thinking skills, thus readying them for arithmetic and scientific processes.
- Numbers are a way to communicate ideas to other people. For the most part, numbers would not be necessary if we did not wish to communicate with other people. Words such as bigger and smaller, more or less are really number words. They tell us how much of something. Arithmetic is the study of numbers.
- Another area of mathematics is the study of shapes. We have two dimensional shapes such as a square and a circle. Three dimensional shapes are spheres and cubes. Mathematics helps to define those shapes. On computers, modern mathematicans are working in multiple dimensions that the human mind cannot comprehend.

Things to do

- While pencil and paper arithmetic skills are inappropriate for the young child, simple measurement using non-standard measures can be very meaningful. Rulers should only be introduced when non-standard measurement has been mastered.
- Bring in materials that contain numbers such as number lines, dice, counting blocks, keyboards, telephone books, and address lists. Discuss the many ways that numbers are used. Cut out numbers and create a number collage.
- Young children need many experiences with comparing real things using words like more, less, most, big, a lot, and so on. Obviously, language and math are closely related.
- Famous mathematicians are Pathagoras, Euclid, Rene Descartes, Kepler, Isaac Newton, Pascal, Gauss, and Albert Einstein.

The following mathematics ideas can be found in:

HUG A TREE

Recording Data
A Piece of Our World
How Many Ways to Grandma's House?
Curves and Straights — The Shapes Nature Makes
I Can Make What You Make
Toss and Find
Count What You Can and Do It Again
The Big Squirt
Measure the Wind
How Do You Measure Things?
Head to Toe All in a Row
The Long and Short of It
Snowjob
Long, Short, Tall, Small — Compare Them All
How Does Your Dandelion Grow?
It Takes a Whole Bunch
Measure Shadows
Fill That Space — An Area Game
How Deep Is Your Snow Drift?
Old and New
Happenings Diary
Water Clocks

MUDPIES TO MAGNETS

Shake, Shake, Shake
Put Them in a Row
Can I Make a Shape?
Zero and Counting
Beans in a Jar
Fill It Up: A Question of Volume
My, How You Have Grown!
Outdoor Hunt and Find
Rain Measures
Stepping Out, Hop, Skip, Jump
The Purr-fect Smell
The Shape and Hop Game

FORTY FOOTPRINTS

Language with science

dry
wet
saturated
count
measure
far
farther
farthest

Things you will need

3 dishes or disposable plates that will hold a small amount of water and are big enough for feet

3 sponges bigger than little feet

cement path

chalk

3 sets of paper and pencils for recording

tape measure

Wet footprints. How far do they go? With practice, the children can become increasingly accurate at predicting the outcome. There is a different outcome with each variable, and the children learn to predict accordingly. And they love running around barefoot!

What to do

1. Place a dry sponge in the first dish. (Label the dish DRY.)

2. Place a damp sponge in the second dish. (Label the dish WET.)

3. Place a very wet sponge in the third dish. (Label the dish SATURATED.)

4. Children step onto the first sponge and step out across the cement to make footprints. (What, no footprints?)

5. Step onto second sponge and walk across the cement; write the child's name with chalk where the last footprint is clear.

6. Repeat with the third sponge. Do the footprints go farther?

7. Let another child try the same procedure. First predict what will happen. How far will the steps go?

8. Keep repeating until all the children have done the series. Add water to dishes as needed.

9. Try one with 3 containers and children side by side. Repeating the results every time is the key to this. If some scientific idea is repeated and is forever predictable, then it becomes a law.

Want to do more?

Measure distances. In another attempt (replication), try to make steps go further. Does it make a difference if you take bigger steps, walk on tiptoes, sides of feet, jump on the sponges to make feet wetter? Predict what will happen, record what does happen, and try new ways of solving the problem. Paint the children's feet and make footprints on mural paper.

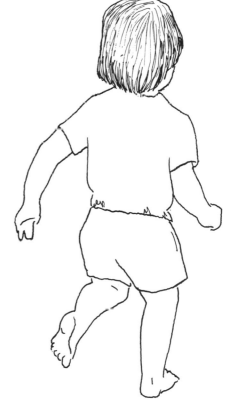

PENNY DROP IN

Language with science

numbers
data sheet
improve

Things you will need

a large clear container (gallon glass jar)

clear glass to sit in larger jar (juice glass)

20-30 pennies
paper
pencil

Water is a liquid. It is a form of matter that conforms to the shape of the object that holds it. Objects can pass through the liquid, but are affected by its presence. Water offers resistance to objects, slows them down, changes their direction. When the object moving through water is not streamlined, it can have its direction changed by the resistance. Drop a few pennies into the water and observe their movement. The problem to be solved here is how to drop the pennies in such a way that they will drop into the cup in the bottom of the jar. Easy? Try it.

What to do

1. Fill the gallon jar with water. Place the small juice glass upright in the bottom.

2. Give the children 10 to 20 pennies. Drop them in the water so they fall in the small glass. Keep a record of the number dropped. How many went into the little glass?

3. Let's try again to see if we can do better. So we can compare our tries, record the number we got in this time on a tally sheet. Children too young to count can make one mark for each penny.

4. Repeat. Count. Record.

5. Repeat. Count. Record.

6. You should be improving your ability to have pennies drop in the glass. Have you figured out the most reliable way to drop a penny and have it go it the glass?

Want to do more?

Try the same activity without water. Is it easier or more difficult? Record your results and find out. Try objects with other shapes — smaller or larger coins, washers, pebbles, shells. See HUG A TREE for more information on using tallies and graphs with young children.

LOOK HOW FAR I CAN JUMP!

Language with science

how far,
measure
count
equal
same
about
long
length
distance

Things you will need

newsprint

blocks of equal
size, drinking
straws

or some other set
of objects equal
in length

Hey! Look how far I jumped! Bet you can't jump that far! How often do children make statements like these? While the numbered markings on a ruler having little meaning for young children, measurement skills can be introduced at a very early age as children make these distance comparisons. Be alert and introduce this activity as an extension of their own play. Just be sure you don't take over and eliminate the fun or the children will quickly lose interest.

What to do

1. Ask the children how far each can jump. Let them show you. If we jump and want to remember how far it was, what could we do? What are their ideas? Measure? With what? We can take a piece of string and make it the same length, then save that string to remember. What is another way? A ruler? Yes, lots of people measure with rulers, but what if we don't have one? What else could we use?

2. Help the children come to the conclusion that they can measure if they have many objects of about the same length that they can line up to equal the distance jumped. Then they can count the number of lined-up objects. Have one of the children jump. Note the starting and ending points. Ask the children to determine which objects in the classroom could be used to keep track of their jumps. The children's choice should be objects that have equal lengths and are plentiful enough to measure the entire

length. Blocks, drinking straws, sheets of paper, or a collection of shoes about the same size will work. Let the children help each other measure their jumps. Record each child's measurement on a newsprint chart with pictures and words such as "Jake jumped 6 shoes."

3. Try it again. Let the children see if they can each make a longer jump. Try to avoid heavy emphasis on who jumps the farthest. The experience should be cooperative and fun, not competition.

Want to do more?

Have Ziploc bags with non-standard units for the children to measure their jumps. The better counters can use smaller objects. If they throw a ball, what should they use to measure? Introduce rulers as standard units. Have them take a set of units home to measure their family's jumps.

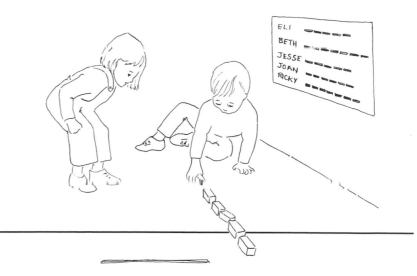

PAIR UP WITH SCIENCE

Language with science

pair
same
similar
match

Things you will need

a set of objects
such as red beans

acorns
elm leaves
hickory nuts
snail shells
oyster shells

or whatever you
find that looks
interesting

set of matching
cards with the
name and picture
of one of these
objects drawn on
each card

You wear a pair of shoes, you wear a pair of socks. When two similiar objects are moved around together, they become a pair. This concept can easily be adapted to include the teaching of science knowledge by using such things as shells, leaves, and insects.

What to do

1. Have the children dump out the objects.

2. Lay the cards face down.

3. Turn the first Pairs Card up. It will be a drawing of one of the objects.

4. Match the card to one of the objects.

5. A pair match is made when you hear the children say they have a pair of (*red beans*).

6. Lay the match on the card and move to next player.

Want to do more?

Change the pairs game cards and objects frequently. This can be done seasonally: nuts in the fall, flowers in the spring, grass seed stalks in late summer. Construct a lotto game by using paired cards. With very young children or those with a limited vocabulary, it can be helpful to introduce the concept of pairs by saying something like, "Let's help each thing find its friend. Yes, they match. You have a pair of shells." For more skilled children, use a collection of objects that requires more attention to detail, such as a group of very similar shells.

HOW MUCH
CAN YOU CARRY?

Language with science

carry
how much
weigh
liter
kilogram
record
more
most
less
bottle
bucket
container

Things you will need

1 liter plastic bottle

two gallon or larger bucket

water source
tally card
pencil

Small children enjoy carrying heavy things. This activity uses the child's need to find and explore individual skills, traits, and limitations while studying and developing early knowledge of mass and volume. Such a deal!

What to do

1. Give the child a bucket and a one liter plastic bottle. Explain that a one liter bottle when full weighs 1 kilogram, or 2.2 pounds.

2. Let the child fill the one liter bottle and pour it into the bucket. Keep a count of the number of bottles. The child is to pour into the bucket the amount that can be carried from one line drawn on the floor to another. (Approximately 3 meters (10 feet) apart.)

3. Let the child carry the bucket. If the child successfully carrys the bucket from one line to the other, record this on the tally sheet with the child's name and the mass/weight of the amount carried. Repeat until the maximum amount is reached.

Want to do more?

Ask what the children feel they might do to help them carry more water at one time, i.e., two buckets, a wagon. Have filled bottles of colored water available for children in the dramatic play area. They love to carry them around. You can glue on the lids so they won't spill.

SERIAL CEREAL

Language with science

serial
cereal
boxes
sequence
order
arrange
property
common
large
small
short
tall
big
little
thick
thin

Things you will need

cereal boxes of
various sizes

One aspect of classification is being able to order objects by an attribute. Because many children have favorite cold cereals and the boxes are readily available, they make excellent subjects for serial ordering. Record how many different ways you can order the boxes.

What to do

1. Arrange a number of cereal boxes on a table in mixed order of size.

2. Have the children serial order the cereal boxes in order of size from tallest to shortest.

3. Rearrange. Let the children choose other ways to order the boxes. Thick to thin, heaviest to lightest according to printed package weight, longest to shortest name...

Want to do more?

With very young children begin with 2 or 3 boxes. Add more as appropriate. Divide into groups — sweetened/unsweetened, round/not round, wheat/oats/corn/mixed...

SCHOOL MAP PUZZLE

Language with science

map
far
near
around
next to
beside

Things you will need

paper
glue

crayons or
markers
scissors

An awareness of maps and their use as models for actual objects is of value to young children. This activity helps them build their first map. It's of something they know and see every day. Precise map making is not the object. Our purpose is to show that maps exist, that children can make them, and that they represent real places.

What to do

1. Draw a large picture of the school yard. On the map, place the big items such as the building, the fence, major trees, sidewalks.

2. With the children, choose the most prominent spots in the yard — slide, tires, swings, and so on — and locate where they are on the map.

3. Have the children draw the objects on paper and cut them out.

4. Orient the map, putting it at the true, cardinal direction. It is best if you can do this outside where the real objects are.

5. Glue the pictures on the map, checking on the placement by looking at the school yard.

Want to do more?

Make a map of another yard, the park, the school, a school room. Have the parents help the children make a map of their rooms at home. Then they could bring the room maps for story time.

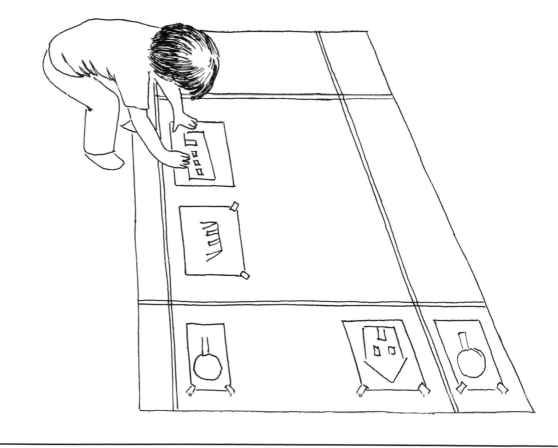

MAKE A BALANCE

Language with science

balance
fulcrum
more
less
weight
compare
light
heavy

Things you will need

a 30 cm (1 ft) piece of a broom handle

a board about 60 cm (2 ft) long for a base

a ruler
a nail
paper clip
a wood screw
string
2 butter tubs

These instructions will help you create an inexpensive balance. It will not be precisely accurate, but it can be used by children for general weighing and comparing. There are endless ways to use a balance. Try this one and you can just turn children loose with a set of things to compare. It's fun!

What to do
Create your balance following these directions:

1. Pound a small nail into the broom handle 2 to 3 cm (1 in) from the top. The nail should be strong enough to hold the ruler and objects to weigh.

2. Attach the base to the upright using the wood screw. Splitting the upright with the screw could happen. Try using a drill to make a hole for the screw.

3. Make a hole in the center of the ruler if it doesn't have one. Place the ruler on the nail. It should balance. If it doesn't, use a paper clip and move it along the light edge until it balances.

4. Tie 3 strings of equal length onto each butter tub.

5. Put everything together as in the picture.

6. Let the children weigh whatever they like. How many different things can they find that weigh about the same?

Want to do more?
Pour sand into film canisters. Label with marker. Find out which is heaviest. Order from heaviest to lightest. Make more canisters that will fit between the ones the children have ordered. The correct order for heavy to light could spell out **weigh**.

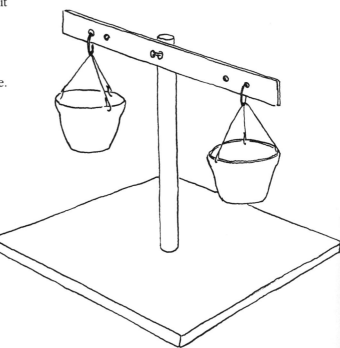

ON THE TRAIL OF FIVES

Language with science

count
find
number
trail
follow
group

Things you will need

objects from out of doors grouped in fives

cardboard hands to be used as pointers

We all know that rote memorization of number concepts does not ensure understanding. Children learn best by doing and re-doing activities that reinforce the concept of numbers. This activity presents a delightful approach to teaching number concepts. We've used five for our example. Choose a number for your group that is right for them.

What to do

1. Prepare a trail for the children to explore. A straight sidewalk or circular path would be easy to use.

2. Prepare the stations. Here are some possibilities: piles of leaves, sticks, rocks, feathers, pine cones, seed pods, sweet gum balls, grass, weeds, dandelions.

3. Prepare the 5's walk by placing a pointing finger above each station.

4. Talk with the children about the number 5. Count the number of fingers and toes. Count to 5.

5. Take the children to the 5's trail. Show them the finger pointer and how it points to a trail.

6. Go from pointer to pointer. Count out five objects at each pointer. What are they called? Why are they all alike? What makes them alike?

7. Go through all the stations.

8. Return to the classroom. See if the class can remember all the stations. What did they find at all the stations? The teacher should list the stations on a large piece of paper as they are remembered.

Want to do more?

Use different numbers and new stations. Create a 1-10 trail.

VOLUME MATCH

Language with science

container
volume
more
less
equal

Things you will need

film canisters
coffee cups
various sized containers
tongue depressors with names

Every experience we can give children in estimating and confirming estimations is a step in improving problem solving skills. The study of volume is one that is not frequently used in schools, even with adults. Some researchers estimate that over half of the population is unable to accurately predict volume. This low ability is probably related to a lack of experience with using volume. This activity is one way to give children experiences with volume. It is something to add to the more common activities focused around water and sand tables.

What to do

1. Write each child's name on a tongue depressor.

2. Explain that the purpose of this game is to find objects in the school yard that can fit inside a container and fill it up. We scientists say it has the same volume as our container.

3. Your job is to look at a container, place your tongue depressor in the container to mark the one you choose, and go out to find an object that fills it up as close as possible. This is a very difficult task because you must hold in your mind a certain size container. You may want to put your hand inside to have a basis for comparison.

4. Okay. Everybody who is trying to match their container volume, go find your object.

5. When they return, check who has been successful and if their object has a volume of more, less, or equal to the container they chose.

6. Choose a different container and go again.

7. Depending on the experience of the children, you may want to begin this activity by allowing them to take the containers with them, then graduate to carrying a mental image of the volume.

Want to do more?

Do the same activity with two dimensional shapes and find objects that have the same area. Collect containers of different shapes that hold the same volume, and experiment with liquids or dried beans.

HOW MANY EQUALS EQUAL?

Language with science

compare
how many
how much
more
less
weigh
the same
equal

Things you will need

an equal arm balance (See "Make a Balance" in this chapter)

cup of rice

blocks
beans
paper clips
bottle caps
washers
paper
pencil

An equal arm balance is often used in science experiments to compare masses of objects. (See "Make a Balance" in this chapter for balance construction.) Objects that are about the same mass, i.e., paper clips, crackers, and bottle caps, can be used to experiment with predictions and comparisons as well as addition and subtraction. The eventual outcome of this activity is learning the concept that to maintain balance, operations carried out on one idea have to be matched by similar operations on the other side.

What to do

1. Place equal arm balance on the table so it is accessible to children.

2. Put one cup of rice on one side of the balance.

3. Distribute blocks to children. How many blocks do you think this cup of rice weighs? Children estimate — then actually place blocks on the other side of the balance until a balance is achieved. Record estimates; compare to final results.

4. Repeat with various items, i.e., beans, bottle caps, washers, etc.

Want to do more?

Place objects on both sides of the balance. How many blocks will we have to take off the first side to have both sides balance?

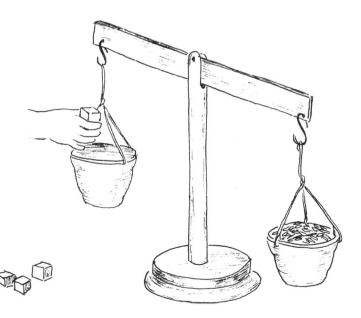

SYMMETRY

Language with science

symmetry
symmetrical
asymmetrical

Things you will need

mirrors
leaves

Symmetrical
leaves
   Crab apple
   Sycamore
   Maple
   Apple
   Orange
   Banana

Asymmetrical
leaves
   Elms
   Oak
   Eucalyptus

Experimenting with symmetry is a way to develop spatial concepts that can enhance careers in art, architecture, and mathematics. The key to this activity is to match up the whole leaf by comparing the mirror images each child makes to the whole leaf. Move the mirror on the leaf to see if the whole leaf can be made every way the mirror can be placed. Mirror cards can also be purchased from school or math and science supply catalogs.

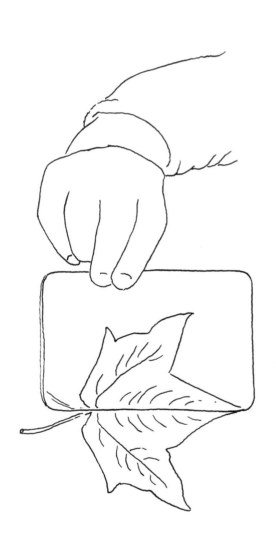

What to do

1. Give the children mirrors.

2. Have them explore the mirror as a tool for reflecting images. Look at their own reflections.

3. Show the children how to lay the mirror on a leaf half so the reflection makes a whole leaf. When this reflection is identical to the whole, you have symmetrical form. Have a paired leaf to make the comparison.

4. Place a number of leaves out for each child to experiment with.

5. Present some asymmetrical leaves to compare.

Want to do more?

Try fruit halves to create a whole fruit. Make symmetrical designs with blocks. Fold painted paper in half to make symmetrical pictures.

ESTIMATION

Language with science

estimate
guess
measure
grow
length
grass
more
less

Things you will need

grass seed
potting soil
plastic cups
tongue depressors
colored markers

Plant growth is a predictable event. Although growth depends on many factors — warmth, water, food, sunlight — when those are kept constant, growth will occur. Because change in an object is not always easy for children to observe, the events in this activity are very necessary. The children involved in estimating grass growth will all have had experiences in seeing grass growth after and before mowing, so they know it grows. How much and how fast are other issues. You could do this activity after mowing the yard or you can grow grass in a cup, estimate, then measure growth.

What to do

1. Plant grass seed in a cup.

2. Let the children estimate how tall they think the grass will grow in 5 days by making a mark on a tongue depressor.

3. Do the same using a different colored mark for the estimate of growth in 10 days.

4. Mark the actual growth with a green mark and number.

5. Compare the marks. How good was your estimate?

Want to do more?

Estimate the growth of other plants. "Mow" the grass. Does it grow faster or slower after mowing? What happens to the grass if you don't water it? What if it gets no sunlight?

HODGE PODGE

MAKE A SIPHON

Children are fascinated when they watch a container filled with water moved by a siphon. Here's how to make it. (To be used with "Water Movers" activity in the **First Physics** chapter.)

What to do
1. Fill one jar or pail with water and place on a table.

2. Place a second jar on a chair so that it is lower than the first.

3. Fill a 100 cm (1 yard) piece of plastic tubing with water. Do this by holding the tube under water until it is filled.

4. Now pinch one end of the tube tightly or hold a finger over the end.

5. Hold the other end in the bottom of the jar while moving the water-filled tube to the lower jar. Release the pressure by removing your fingers from the ends of the tube.

The water will flow from the jar on the table to the jar on the chair. This happens because there is more water in the long arm of the tube then in the short arm. Gravity acts on the long arm and the water runs out leaving a partial vacuum in the tube. This way water is transferred continuously from one jar to another.

Another way to start the siphon — a way that will be easier for the children — is to

1. Put one end of the tube in the jar of water on the table.

2. Now, suck the air from the lower end of the tube. This will also create a partial vacuum and the water will flow.

Want to do more?
Select tubes of varying diameters to experiment with. Does the water move faster or slower? Do the different diameter tubes present problems in their use?

SAND CLOCK

There are many different types of clocks, but they are all used to measure time. The clock in this activity is a sand clock. Make it and see how long it takes to fill one bottle of sand from another (approximately 3 minutes). You can use it over and over to measure how much time it takes to set the table, put on your coat, pick up your toys, or whatever else you can think of to do.

Language with science

time
timer
turn over
liter
minute
clock

Things you will need

2 two liter soda bottles

2 liters of dry sand

film canisters
washer (1 inch)

What to do

1. Fill a two liter bottle full of dry sand.

2. Follow the directions given in "Tornado Tower" in the **Weather Watchers** chapter to construct a connector.

3. Connect the full bottle to the empty one. It should all fit together snugly.

4. Turn sand-filled bottle to the top and time.

5. Mississippi river sand (quite fine) takes 3 minutes to empty.

Want to do more?

Try different sand. Use the sand clock to measure how long something takes to do. Calibrate the clock by 30-second intervals or one-minute intervals.

BUG CATCHER

Flies are relatively easy to find in all seasons except for winter. The children can have great fun as they attempt to capture them and keep them for experimenting as in "Cool Off a Fly" in the **Animal Adventures** chapter. A bug catcher can be easily made using a clear plastic cup, a piece of paper, and a peanut butter jar. The child quickly places the cup over the bug. Slide a piece of paper under the cup. Now turn the cup over, keeping it covered with the piece of paper. Place a peanut butter jar over the upturned cup. Remove the paper. The bug will attempt to escape. It will crawl or fly upward, hopefully, into the jar. Place lid with air holes on the jar. The bug is captured!

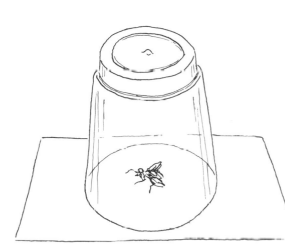 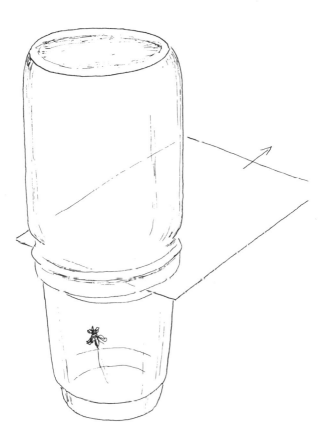

RAINBOW CATCHER

What to do

1. Using string, connect 6 pieces of straw as shown in the illustration. The string can be pushed or sucked through the straw.

2. Cut out triangles of yellow, red, and blue cellophane to fit the triangles in the straw structure. Plastic term paper covers work well.

3. Use model or super glue to glue the cellophane to the tetrahedron.

5. Where the strings join add a hanger.

6. Place in a sunny window to catch the light.

Want to do more?

The cellophane in the triangles filters light, letting only certain types of light through. You should be able to move the Rainbow Catcher in the light and achieve a variety of colors. How does this fit with other color activities you have done?

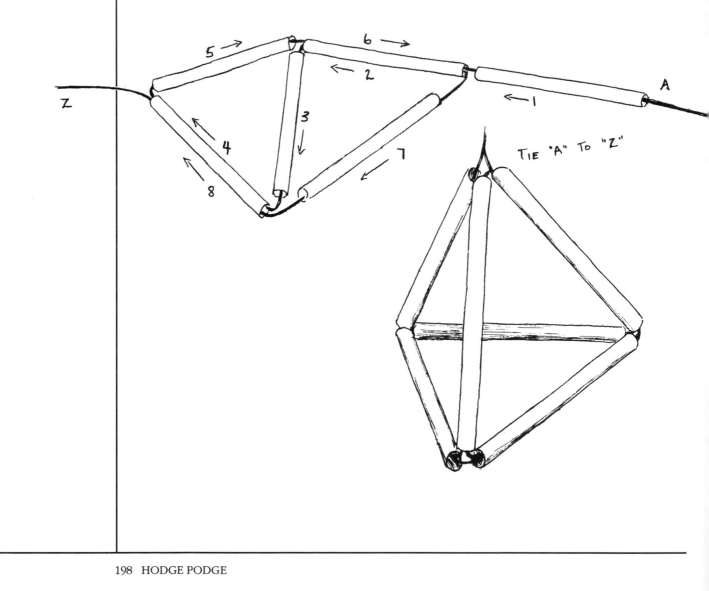

TIE "A" TO "Z"

INDEX

Story S-t-r-e-t-c-h-e-r-s:
Activities to Expand Children's Favorite Books

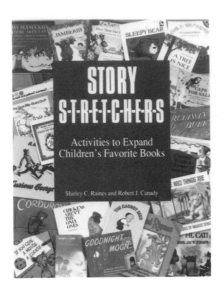

Shirley C. Raines and Robert J. Canady

Children love to hear and look at good books. Here is a perfect way to connect children's enthusiasm for books with other areas of the curriculum. *Story S-t-r-e-t-c-h-e-r-s* are teaching plans based on the stories in outstanding picture books that are among children's favorites.

Here are 450 teaching ideas to expand the interest of 90 different books. These ideas are organized around eighteen units commonly taught in the early childhood classroom.

"*Story S-t-r-e-t-c-h-e-r-s* is the best thing to happen to story time in decades. It should be the bible of every preschool and early primary teacher in America. Even better, it can be used just as easily by parents. Nothing I've seen approaches it in practicality and originality."—Jim Trelease, Author of *The New Read Aloud Handbook*

ISBN 0-87659-119-5

Mudpies to Magnets:
A Preschool Science Curriculum

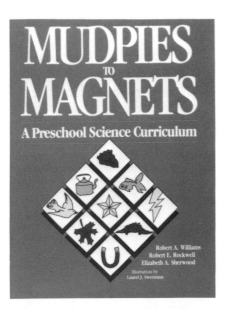

Robert A. Williams, Robert E. Rockwell, and Elizabeth A. Sherwood, Illus. Laurel Sweetman

Here are 112 ready-to-use science experiments. Each one provides fascinating, hands-on learning activities which young children can experience themselves. The units include *Science Center Activities, Construction and Measurement, Circle Time Activities, Scientific Art, Science for a Special Place, Health and Nutrition, Outdoor Science,* and *Creativity and Movement.*

Each experiment includes a clear explanation of what happens, a list of words to use for language development, a list of things you will need, a description of what to do, and suggestions of additional ways to extend the activity.

ISBN 0-87659-112-8

The Learning Circle:
A Preschool Teacher's Guide to Circle Time

Patty Claycomb

Hundreds of circle time activities make this a necessary book. Activities can be used again and again because they give children a chance to talk about themselves and their friends. There are learning circle activities for every month, day, and season. Patty Claycomb knows how to weave a spirit of magic and adventure into the daily classroom.

ISBN 0-87659-115-2

Do Touch: Instant, Easy, Hands-On
Learning Experiences for Young Children

LaBritta Gilbert

This unique book of hands-on activities is designed to surround children with things to explore, wonder about, do and discover. These activities can be prepared quickly and easily from simple materials such as cups, sponges, craft sticks, corks, rice, and sandpaper. The chapters focus on pairing and puzzling, forming, fitting, categorizing, measuring, sorting and more. Clear directions and objectives are aided by expert illustrations.

ISBN 0-87659-118-7